An Outdoor Gas Griddle Cookbook

Sizzling Recipes for Open-Air Culinary Adventures on Your Gas Griddle

James Murray

Table of Content

ESSENTIALS OF OUTDOOR GAS GRIDDLE OPERATION

A griddle is a flat cooking device, often made of cast iron or stainless steel, utilized for grilling purposes. Its defining feature is a consistent heat source that can be sustained for extended periods. During this method of controlled heating, browning takes place and the Maillard reaction, a cooking phenomenon, unlocks various flavors and aromas from the food. This is particularly noticeable in meats, but is also present in bread, roasted coffee, pastries, and onions.

A griddle comprises a grilling surface embedded with multiple heating elements. Each of these elements is independently controlled. The heating of the cooking surface can be achieved using electricity or propane, but propane is typically preferred for its more uniform heat distribution.

Cast iron or stainless steel is often used for the cooking surface as they retain heat effectively and can be swiftly reheated as required. This attribute becomes more pronounced with increased thickness of the steel. Moreover, the individual heating elements allow for the creation of different temperature zones on a potentially expansive cooking surface.

Griddles are manufactured in both floor-standing and countertop models. Some models are even designed to be placed on top of existing stoves. Floor models often utilize stainless steel due to its ease of cleaning. Additionally, removing fat from the griddle's edges serves as a precautionary measure to avoid unnecessary burning of excess grease.

A well-designed grease trap ensures that oil drainage is simple and quick, and some griddles feature grooves on the cooking surface to aid in oil drainage whilst simultaneously grilling food.

A griddle is designed for ease of use. The manufacturer has created numerous accessories to accompany the griddle, but there are several essential components that come with an outdoor gas griddle:

Griddle top: This is where the cooking takes place. It's made of steel and sloped to prevent juices from interfering with the cooking process. The griddle top is heated to the required cooking temperature over multiple burners. · Side shelf: This is attached to the griddle and can be used for storing seasonings and other cooking ingredients. It is not designed to hold heavy items. · Foldable legs and wheels: These features allow the griddle to be easily moved. Thanks to the caster wheels, the griddle can be positioned exactly where you want it and features a lock mechanism to prevent unwanted movement. · Drip dish: This collects the juices produced during cooking. The griddle top is angled so any liquid on its surface runs into the drip dish through a small steel tube. · Removable drip tray: Located at the bottom of the grill between the movable legs, it assists with fluid collection when the volume of juice is large. · Control valves: These control the heat for all griddle cooking. They are used to regulate the temperature of the burners.

Ignition switch: Pressing this battery-operated, self-contained button ignites the outdoor gas griddle. The griddle then starts to heat up to the temperature you've selected using the control valve.

HOW IT WORKS

The method of operation for a griddle is similar to traditional griddle cooking - both involve heating a flat surface for cooking. However, unlike traditional griddles, this griddle does not require the cooking surface to be removed from direct heat, as it has temperature control valves. It creates a controlled flame using propane or butane LPG bottle gas as fuel. The griddle is set to a specific temperature using the control valves and ignited using the built-in igniter needles that light the burner tube. This tube, located beneath the griddle top, is responsible for maintaining the correct temperature.

Food is cooked directly on the heated griddle top, unlike in traditional griddle cooking. The griddle's heat allows for frying, broiling, and searing. Here's a step-by-step guide on how to ignite the griddle:

1. Ensure that the battery in the ignition switch is correctly installed.
2. Open the control valve on the gas cylinder and the control valve on the gas bottle to release the gas.
3. Turn the control valves on the griddle until the indicator line on the griddle points to "high."
4. Press the ignition switch promptly. You should hear a clicking sound. Prior to cooking each meal, preheat the griddle for 3–5 minutes.

In this method, the griddle uses the propane or butane LPG bottle gas as a fuel source and is ready to cook your meal. The griddle top's heating process, along with the various control and maintenance features, make the outdoor gas griddle an efficient and versatile cooking appliance. Whether you're searing steaks or frying eggs, the griddle provides a consistent and controllable heat source to ensure your food is cooked to perfection.

SETTING UP THE GRIDDLE

After unboxing your Outdoor Gas Griddle, refer to the user guide to confirm that all components and fasteners are present. For assembly, ensure the griddle is on a flat surface

 (to prevent it from rolling away) and follow these steps: First, verify that the battery in the ignition switch is properly installed. Attach the propane gas cylinder securely to the gas line. Activate the gas and release it through the gas control valve. Ignite your griddle by pressing the gas control valve and the ignition switch until you hear the flame. For best cooking performance, preheat the griddle for 3– 5 minutes before adding food. Now your griddle is ready for cooking whatever you'd like.

CONTROLLING YOUR GRIDDLE

The Outdoor Gas Griddle comes with user-friendly controls that will haveyou cooking in no time.

Ignition button: This battery-powered button lights your griddle. Press, hold, and the leftmost burner will ignite.

Left burner knob: Turn it clockwise to adjust the heat on the left burner.

Left-center burner knob: Turn it clockwise to increase the heat on the left-center burner.

Right-center burner knob: Turn it clockwise to raise the heat on the right-center burner.

Right burner knob: Turn it clockwise to increase the heat on the right burner.

GRIDDLING PROCESS

Here are several critical steps to follow before placing your food on the grill for optimal cooking results:

1. Preheat the Grill: Preheating your gas grill is essential for even cooking and preventing food from sticking to the grates. Turn on the grill and adjust it to the desired temperature. Allow it to preheat for 10 to 15 minutes, ensuring it reaches the correct temperature before cooking.

2. Clean the Grates: Use a grill brush or scraper to thoroughly clean the grates. This removes any leftover food particles or debris from previous grilling sessions, ensuring a clean surface for your food and preventing unwanted flavors.

3. Oil the Grates: To prevent food from sticking, lightly oil the grates. Fold a paper towel to make a small pad, saturate it with cooking oil, and then use tongs to rub the oiled towel across the grates. This creates a non-stick surface and makes it easier to flip food when needed.

4. Prepare the Food: Season or marinate your food as desired. Ensure that meats are at room temperature before grilling to promote even cooking. Cut vegetables or other ingredients to the desired size and thickness for optimal grilling results.

5. Adjust Heat Zones: If your gas grill has multiple burners, create different heat zones by adjusting the heat intensity. This allows for a hotter section for searing and a cooler section for slower cooking or keeping food warm. Searing meat and cooking veggies on high is recommended. However, low heat should never be used to cook meat on the Outdoor Gas Griddle as it can overheat the surface and make the griddle brittle, potentially causing various types of damage. When cooking eggs, remember that Outdoor Gas Griddle recommends using medium heat.

6. Heat setting: Searing meat and cooking veggies on high is recommended. However, low heat should never be used to cook meat on the Outdoor Gas Griddle as it can overheat the surface and make the griddle brittle, potentially causing various types of damage.

7. Place food on the Griddle: Carefully place the prepared food on the preheated griddle. You can achieve attractive griddle marks for meats by placing them at a diagonal angle to the grates.

8. Avoid Overcrowding: Leave enough space between items when grilling to ensure even cooking by distributing the heat evenly. If necessary, cook in batches or use a second griddle to accommodate larger quantities of food.

9. Flip at the Right Time: Flip the food only when it releases easily from the grates. If the food sticks, it likely needs more time to cook before flipping. Meat should be flipped once to prevent it from drying out.

10. Check Doneness: Use a food thermometer to accurately check the internal temperature of meats to ensure they are cooked to a safe level. Refer to a reliable cooking chart to determine the right temperatures for different types of meat.

11. Rest the Meat: After removing meat from the grill, allow it to rest for a few minutes before cutting. This allows the juices to redistribute, resulting in a moister, more flavorful meal.

12. Clean After Each Use: After you finish grilling, while the griddle is still hot, scrape off any food residue with a grill brush or scraper. Occasionally, deep clean the griddle by applying some water and scraping it off to remove stubborn grease and food particles.

CLEANING YOUR GRIDDLE

Maintaining your griddle after each use is essential, yet its cleaning procedure differs from typical cookware. Dish soap, usually beneficial for removing grease, is not advised here as it interferes with the griddle's seasoning layer. Instead, a restaurant-style cleaning approach is recommended – employing a griddle scraper and hot water. A griddle scraper can effectively get rid of residual food particles without harming your seasoning layer. Hot water is effective at dissolving most fats and sauces that can then be scraped off. While a routine deep-clean isn't a must, re-seasoning your grill after cleaning can help preserve its gleaming, dark finish.

Frequent griddle users should clean their equipment regularly to avoid flavor contamination from burnt oil and residue, and to maintain efficiency. Proper cleaning typically takes about 5-10 minutes – starting from the top of the grill and working down to the grease trough. By moving food around on the grill or rubbing the grate after each use, you can make maintenance easier and prevent food from sticking.

To maintain the grill's performance, oil your griddle each time you use it, wiping off residue with a soft cloth after each use. Applying a thin layer of oil isn't the same as seasoning your griddle, which we'll discuss in a later post. After washing and drying your griddle, apply a thin layer of oil with a paper towel while it's still warm to prevent rusting.

SAFETY GUIDELINES

Leak Prevention Always ensure there are no leaks before using your griddle. Mix soap and water in a cup and gently pour it over the hose and all parts connecting the griddle to the propane tank. Then, turn on your tank. If bubbles appear at the connection point, it indicates a leak. If not, you're good to go. In case of leaks, turn off your tank immediately and contact your Outdoor Gas Griddle supplier or your local fire department for assistance.

Reignition Care If your griddle fails to ignite despite pressing the igniter, wait for 5 minutes before trying again. When you turn on your propane tank, the gas fills up your griddle immediately, and needs a few minutes to dissipate. Failing to do so can cause flare-ups. If you're still unsuccessful after the third try, get in touch with your supplier immediately.

Temperature Checks Check the temperature by placing your hand 6 inches from the griddle's center — if it's too hot to hold your hand there for more than two seconds, it's ready to cook. Alternatively, you could use a thermometer placed 9 inches from the center of the Outdoor Gas Griddle.

CHOOSING THE RIGHT OUTDOOR GAS GRIDDLE

When most people think of a griddle, they picture a small, plug-in countertop appliance or a large diner-style flat top. The modern gas griddle combines the convenience of a propane grill with the functionality of a griddle, resulting in a versatile, portable cooking tool.

Outdoor Gas Griddle griddles are loved for their quality and variety. Whether you need an all-in-one solution for backyard cooking or a portable option for camping, a Outdoor Gas Griddle fits the bill. The standard 36-inch cooking station includes a side shelf and four independent heat zones, producing up to 60,000 BTUs — enough to cook 72 hotdogs and 28 hamburgers simultaneously.

For those who need a portable option, there's the 22-inch tabletop griddle, capable of reaching 24,000 BTUs with two 'H' style burners and a hood to keep the surface clean. A 17-inch portable model is also available for those who wish to cook in more remote locations.

If you're attached to traditional griddle cooking methods, hybrid models are available too. For instance, the griddle and charcoal grill combo lets you experiment with griddling while still enjoying traditional charcoal grilling. There's also a griddle and a tabletop air fryer model. If you've always wanted to bring your deep fryer outdoors, this is your chance. These hybrid models are perfect if you're looking for a combination of outdoor cooking methods.

Each model caters to specific needs and situations. Consider the frequency and volume of your cooking, the kind of food you'll be making, and the locations where you'll be using the griddle, before making a decision. Whichever model you choose, the versatility of a Outdoor Gas Griddle will enhance your outdoor cooking experience.

DIFFERENCE BETWEEN GRIDDLE AND GRILL

Griddles (flat or raised) distribute heat from the metal surface to the food more evenly. In contrast, grills allow food to cook directly over the heat source.

A grill's bars are typically steel, whereas a griddle has a nonstick flat surface.

Griddles are, without a doubt, easier to use than grills, but they are much slower than professional (gas-fire) grills.

The griddle's large surface area allows you to cook more food simultaneously. In contrast, the grill's small surface area often encourages you to cook less.

Thus, the griddle wins due to its flat surface, which provides more cooking space and is easier to clean.

HOW TO SELECT THE BEST OUTDOOR GAS GRIDDLE GRILL

There are three types of Outdoor Gas Griddle grills on the market right now: flat, dome, and hinged. The most common type is the flat grill, which has grown in popularity due to its easy cleaning. However, one disadvantage of this grill is that it cooks at a lower temperature than a dome or hingedgrill. The other two styles have more in common (both domed) but also have a few distinct differences that set them apart.

A Smoke Hollow Large Camacho Grill is an example of a high-quality hinge-style cooker. The Big Green Egg, Camp Chef, Char-Broil, and the Smoke Vault Double Master Q are other examples of this type of grill.

A dome-style cooker is best for things that need to be evenly cooked. Here's an illustration: Crispy Pork Loin Dome cookers have the advantage of being surface-coated with ceramic, which allows them to reach higher temperatures than flat or hinged models. However, the disadvantage of this design is that it is more difficult to clean because the heat has nowhere to go but down onto the cooking surface, collecting and eventually burning off the grease. Here are a few dome style cooker examples: The Big Green Egg, Napoleon, Camp Chef, Montana Sport, and Brinkmann are a few examples.

Another type of Outdoor Gas Griddle grill worth mentioning is portable. Unfortunately, this cooker does not live up to its name because it contains cast iron components that cannot be heated to the same temperatures as the other two styles. However, because it uses charcoal briquettes, it has advantages over similar propane or electricity cookers. The disadvantage is that charcoal is more expensive than propane and takes much longer to heat up. Portable grills are convenient for tailgating or picnics as they are easily transportable and can be used in a variety of locations. If you want to achieve that authentic Outdoor Gas Griddle flavor, you might be tempted to buy one, but I recommend waiting until you can afford a flat or hinged- style cooker.

WHICH SIZE OUTDOOR GAS GRIDDLE GRILLSHOULD I BUY?

Smaller grills are ideal for people who cook in smaller quantities and have limited space.

The medium-sized grill is ideal for families or couples who want to cook in larger quantities or require more space.

Finally, large Outdoor Gas Griddle grills cater to large groups of people who enjoy cooking large quantities at once and require more space to do so effectively.

BENEFITS OF USING OUTDOOR GAS GRIDDLE OUTDOOR GAS GRIDDLE

When selecting the right cooking equipment for a BBQ enthusiast, the stakes are high. Will you stick with a traditional grill or try out the newcomer, the griddle? Both cookers serve essentially the same purpose and can prepare the same foods. That is why deciding whether or not to purchase a griddle can be perplexing. In this section, you'll learn about the benefits and drawbacks of a grill and how it compares to a standard grill to know whether a griddle is the best option for you. But first, let's go over the fundamentals of grilling.

Griddles are a popular choice for restaurants and other establishments that must quickly and efficiently prepare large quantities of food. Furthermore, using a griddle is a great way to cook healthier because it allows you to prepare food without oil or fat.

Here are some of the health advantages of using a griddle:

- **You consume less fat**. Cooking on a griddle is a convenient and healthy way to prepare food because it requires little—if any—fat. In addition, excess oil drips off the grates and collects in a tray beneath the food. This one significantly reduces the amount of fat you consume.

- **Cooking on a large and flat surface**. The large and flat cooking surface of the Outdoor Gas Griddle gas griddle is one of its main advantages. The large cooking area allows you to cook more food at once, and flipping food is more straightforward than a frying pan. You can cook a large amount of food on the griddle. The Outdoor Gas Griddle can hold 72 hotdogs, 28 hamburgers, and 16 steaks in a single cooking batch. The large cooking surface does not retain moisture and produces a crispy cooking result. It is an excellent choice for larger families who enjoy eggs, bacon, hotdogs, burgers, and vegetables at backyard parties.

- **Excellent construction quality**. The Outdoor Gas Griddle gas grills are constructed of high-quality stainless steel. The primary cooking surface is made of high-quality 7-gauge rolled steel. The entire body surface is protected from rust by a black powder coating.

- **It is powered by propane gas**. The Outdoor Gas Griddle gas grills cook your food with propane gas. Unlike charcoal, propane gas does not produce smoke or harmful gases when cooking food in your backyard. Propane griddles are simple; turn the dial to get the burner going. The gas griddle can keep a consistent temperature. Your griddle takes lessthan 15 minutes to reach its maximum temperature.

- **Versatile**. The Outdoor Gas Griddle is ideal for making everything from delicate fish patties to hearty biscuits. Plus, it's useful for more than just cooking: use your griddle to serve or keep food warm until it's ready to be served in a buffet setting. It also functions as a prep table, with plenty of room

for slicing, dicing, and preparing ingredients. The Outdoor Gas Griddle gas griddle is a versatile outdoor cooking appliance that can cook most foods on a smooth cooking surface. The Outdoor Gas Griddle gas griddle has four burners that can be controlled independently.

- **Simple to clean**. One of the simplest tasks is to clean the greasy cooking area of the Outdoor Gas Griddle. To clean grease, use a spatula or griddle to scrape it up. Wipe down the cooking surface with a paper towel before finishing with a scouring pad. The 10-inch-thick all-steel construction will withstand the most demanding jobs while remaining surprisingly simple to clean with soap and water.

- **A system with two sealed burners**. Heavy stainless-steel grates protect your countertop from scorching accidents such as grease fires or intense heat. The Outdoor Gas Griddle griddle's dual burner system allowsyou to cook on both sides simultaneously.

- **Multi-purpose**. A Outdoor Gas Griddle Griddle's surface area can more than double that of a standard fryer pan or grilling grate, allowing you to simultaneously cook more of your signature items. That means spending less time in the kitchen and more time with your family.

- **Outstanding design**. The thick, heavy cooking surface and closed system design of the Outdoor Gas Griddle prevent flare-ups by preventing flames from spreading from burner to burner. The system also eliminates exposure to open flames, reducing the possibility of accidents involving hot grease or vaporized cooking oil.

TIME-TEMPERATURE RELATIONSHIP IN COOKING PHASE

The most frequently asked question about using a flat-top grill is about temperature, but it's more complex than it appears. Cooking on a flat-top grill is unlike baking cake in the oven. There's more to it than just baking for 30 minutes at 350°F. The reaction of your food will tell you whether the temperature of your flat-top grill was too high or too low. So, what exactly do I mean?

When cooking on a gas grill, mastering the art of perfect cooking times is essential to achieve delicious and succulent results. The cooking times for various foods on a gas grill can vary depending on factors such as the thickness of the food, desired doneness, and the grill's temperature.

For thinner cuts of meat like burgers, hot dogs, and vegetables, shorter cooking times ranging from 8 to 12 minutes at medium-high heat are typically sufficient.

However, thicker cuts such as steaks, pork chops, and chicken breasts may require longer cooking times, usually between 12 to 20 minutes, depending on the desired level of doneness. It is essential to regularly check the internal temperature of meats using a meat thermometer to ensure they reach the appropriate safe temperatures. Additionally, delicate foods like fish or shrimp cook quickly, usually within 4 to 8 minutes, while more oversized items like whole chickens or roasts may require more extended cooking times, often exceeding 1 hour.

Remember, these cooking times serve as general guidelines, and adjusting them based on personal preferences and specific recipes is always recommended for achieving outstanding grilled dishes.

THE CORRECT TEMPERATURE

Determining whether the griddle has reached the correct temperature is crucial for optimal cooking results. Here are a few methods to help you assess if the griddle is adequately heated:

- **Visual Cues**: Observing visual cues is one way to gauge the griddle's temperature. When the griddle is preheated correctly, it will emit light smoke or haze. Those indicate that the cooking surface is hot and ready for use. Additionally, you may notice the griddle surface taking on a slight sheen or glossiness, another indicator of reaching the desired temperature.

- **Water Test**: Another method is the water test. Sprinkle a few drops of water onto the griddle surface. The griddle is likely hot enough if the water droplets sizzle and evaporate almost immediately upon contact. It happens because the water droplets rapidly heat up and disappear on the hot surface.

- **Temperature Gauge**: If your griddle has a built-in temperature gauge, use it as a reliable reference. Set the temperature to the specified level indicated in the recipe or according to your preference and wait for the indicator to reach that temperature. Remember that various recipes may call for different temperature settings, so ensure to make the necessary adjustments accordingly.

- **Time Estimate**: Preheating a griddle typically takes several minutes, depending on the type of griddle and the desired temperature. As a general rule of thumb, most griddles will need approximately 10-15 minutes to reach moderate to high heat. However, it's always best to consult your griddle's instructions for recommended preheating times.

Remember, achieving the correct temperature on a griddle is vital for even cooking and preventing food from sticking. Taking the time to preheat adequately ensures a successful cooking experience and delicious results.

TIPS FOR USING OUTDOOR GAS GRIDDLES

Use Basic Griddle Tools While Cooking Food

Essential griddle accessories such as a spatula, scraper, and squeeze bottles are imperative when utilizing your griddle. Squeeze bottles pour water, oil, and dressing while cooking your food on a griddle, and scrappers and spatulas are used to turn and mix your food.

It's Important to Prepare Food

Before cooking, double-check that you have all the necessary materials and raw foods. There is no time for chopping and cutting your items once the cooking begins. There is a risk of food burning as a result of this. As a result, always have prepared ingredients on hand before starting the cooking procedure.

Cooking Using Extra Tools Is a Good Idea

A basting cover is one of the additional pieces of equipment that aids in steaming, roasting, and melting your meal. A grill press is another piece of equipment that allows you to press your food while cooking to remove excess fat and oils.

Cooking With Water Is a Good Idea

The water will aid in the speedier cooking of your food. Squeeze a small amount of water over a hot griddle surface to create steam, which aids in the quicker cooking of your meal.

Water is helpful while using a griddle, but only some use it. Water removes stuck-on food, cleans the remaining residue, and cooks vegetables.

If you're scraping food off with your scraper and a section is stuck, spray the area with water; the steam will help loosen it up. It will now come off much easier with your scraper when you scrape it off.

Always Preheat the Griddle Before Cooking a Large Meal

It is recommended to preheat the griddle before cooking, especially if you are hosting a gathering or party. It only takes 10 minutes, and the flavor will undoubtedly improve. When placed on a prepared griddle, the oil infuses with the steel and keeps seasoning. This results in a nonstick surface that permits more tasty items to be ready.

Season the Cooking Surface with Salt and Pepper

Seasoning must be used correctly to provide the most excellent cooking outcomes. "What exactly is seasoning?" you might ask. Until nonstick coatings were introduced, there was only one technique to keep food from adhering to the stovetop. Applying a layer of burnt oil will give you a beautiful nonstick finish and help to prevent scratches and oxidation on the cooking surface.

Keep Your Griddle in Use from Season to Season

Because your griddle will most certainly be kept outside, there are a few things you should do before storing it and before using it again after it has been stored. First, unplug the gas tank and store it away from the griddle with the valve closed before storing it. Insects and dust can be kept from the griddle using a griddle cover. When you're ready to use your griddle again, check the burner area for spider webs. If the traps aren't removed before cooking, they may catch fire and cause a flare-up. Next, check your gas tank's level to make sure you have enough to start cooking. Once the tank is connected and you're ready to cook, it's an excellent idea to reseason the cooking surface. Follow the methods outlined above to restore your griddle to its previous splendor.

Invest in the Right Equipment

You'll need professional-grade cooking equipment to get the most out of your griddle. While your kitchen may already have a variety of spatulas, we recommend investing in two long metal spatulas to get the most out of your griddle. These spatulas are durable and can simultaneously transport and turn a large amount of food. They're also thin and flexible, so you can scoop up hash browns without spilling anything. A set of long-handled metal tongs is also recommended because they allow you to reach all areas of the griddle without getting burned.

Experiment With Different Types of Cooking Fats

Unlike some traditional grills, which allow cooking fat to fall into the coals or gas jets, the finest griddles keep cooking grease where it belongs: on your food! It is possible to try different cooking fats to attain the desired outcome. Various oils possess distinct tastes and effects. For example, olive oil adds depth to dishes by providing a strong, sometimes spicy black pepper flavor. The problem with olive oil is its low smoke point, which means it starts to taste burned once it reaches a specific temperature. When cooking at a low to medium temperature, use olive oil; when cooking at a high temperature, avoid it. Choose canola or regular vegetable oil if you want high-heat cooking oil. They'll allow you to cook at high heat without burning the food. Butter has more flavor than anything else but tends to burn, so use it for low-heat or quick cooking foods.

Clean Your Griddle After Each Use

After the first few uses, your griddle will automatically season itself. Cleaning your griddle is an essential component of keeping it clean and sanitary. Using hot water and a paper towel, clean the griddle surface. Do not use soapy water to clean the cooking surface. With a scrapper, clean the stove area. To wipe out the greasy feeling, use clean and dry paper towels.

How to Get Rid of Rust

Scrape any rust spots on the griddle with 40–60 low-grit sandpaper or steel wool to remove them altogether.

Coat the Griddle After Cleaning

Apply a thin coat of cooking spray to the cooking surface after cleaning the griddle to prevent rust from accumulating on the griddle's overcooking surface area.

Storage and Care for Griddles

After cleaning your griddle, place it somewhere cool and dry. To avoid dust, keep your griddle covered and away from humid areas.

TYPICAL GRIDDLE TEMPERATURE CHART

Typical griddle temperatures can vary significantly based on what you're cooking. Here's a general guide to some common foods and the griddle temperature you might use for each:

- Pancakes and French Toast: 350 to 375 degrees Fahrenheit (175 to 190 degrees Celsius).

- Eggs: 250 to 275 degrees Fahrenheit (120 to 135 degrees Celsius).

- Grilled sandwiches: 375 to 400 degrees Fahrenheit (190 to 205 degrees Celsius).

- Burgers and Sausages: 375 to 400 degrees Fahrenheit (190 to 205 degrees Celsius).

- Steak and Chops: 375 to 400 degrees Fahrenheit (190 to 205 degrees Celsius).

- Fish and Seafood: 325 to 350 degrees Fahrenheit (165 to 175 degrees Celsius).

- Vegetables: 375 to 400 degrees Fahrenheit (190 to 205 degrees Celsius).

Keep in mind that these are just rough guidelines and the exact cooking temperature can vary based on your specific recipe or personal preference. It's also important to note that griddles, much like ovens, can have hot spots, so you might need to move your food around to ensure it cooks evenly.

Lastly, always preheat your griddle before you start cooking. This will ensure that your food cooks evenly and helps to achieve a good sear on items like steak and burgers. You can use a griddle thermometer to ensure that your griddle is at the right temperature before you begin cooking.

STEAK DONENESS AND LEVELS

The USDA recommends a minimum internal temperature of 145 degrees Fahrenheit (63 degrees Celsius) for all cuts of beef, including steaks, to ensure safe consumption. However, personal preferences for steak doneness often result in different internal temperatures. Here is a guide to understanding steak doneness levels and their corresponding internal temperatures:

1. **Rare**: The internal temperature should be 120-125 degrees Fahrenheit (49-52 degrees Celsius). This steak will have a bright red, cool center.

2. **Medium Rare**: The internal temperature should be 130-135 degrees Fahrenheit (54-57 degrees Celsius). This steak will be mostly pink with a hint of red in the center and slightly warmer.

3. **Medium**: The internal temperature should be 135-145 degrees Fahrenheit (57-63 degrees Celsius). The center of this steak will be a light pink color.

4. **Medium Well**: The internal temperature should be 145-155 degrees Fahrenheit (63-68 degrees Celsius). This steak will be mostly brown with a slight hint of pink in the center.

5. **Well Done**: The internal temperature should be 155 degrees Fahrenheit (68 degrees Celsius) or higher. A well-done steak is usually completely brown throughout and hotter.

6. Remember, these temperatures refer to the internal temperature of the steak, not the temperature of the griddle or grill. Use a meat thermometer to check the internal temperature to ensure the correct level of doneness.

7. Also, take into account carryover cooking. When a steak is removed from heat, it will continue to cook for a few minutes. This could raise the internal temperature by 5 degrees or more. So, it is often suggested to remove the steak from heat when it's about 5 degrees less than your desired temperature.

BREAKFAST RECIPES

BACON AND GRUYERE OMELET

Difficulty level: Easy

Preparation time: 5 minutes

Cooking time: 15 minutes

Servings: 4

Ingredients:

- 6 eggs, beaten
- 6 strips bacon
- ¼ lb gruyere, shredded
- 1 tsp black pepper
- 1 tsp salt
- 1 tbsp chives, finely chopped
- 1 tsp vegetable oil

Directions:

1. Add salt to the beaten eggs and set aside for 10 minutes.
2. Heat your griddle to medium heat and add the bacon strips. Cook until most of the fat has been rendered, but bacon is still flexible. Remove the bacon from the griddle and place it on paper towels.
3. Once the bacon has drained, chop it into small pieces.
4. Add the eggs to the griddle in two even pools. Cook until the bottom of the eggs starts to firm up. Add the gruyere to the eggs and cook until the cheese has started to melt and the eggs are just starting to brown.

5. Add the bacon pieces and use a spatula to turn one half of the omelet onto the other half.

6. Remove from the griddle, season with pepper and chives, and serve.

SAUSAGE AND VEGETABLE SCRAMBLE

Difficulty level: Hard

Preparation time: 10 minutes

Cooking time: 20 minutes

Servings: 4

Ingredients:

- 8 eggs, beaten
- ½ lb sausage, sliced into thin rounds or chopped
- 1 green bell pepper, sliced
- 1 yellow onion, sliced
- 1 cup white mushrooms, sliced
- 1 tsp salt
- ½ tsp black pepper
- 1 tbsp Vegetable oil

Directions:

1. Preheat the griddle to medium-high heat.
2. Brush the griddle with vegetable oil and add peppers and mushrooms. Cook until lightly browned and then add the onions. Season with salt and pepper and cook until the onions are soft.
3. Add the sausage to the griddle and mix with the vegetables. Cook until lightly browned.
4. Add the eggs, mix with the vegetables and cook until the eggs reach the desired doneness. Use a large spatula to remove the scramble from the griddle and serve immediately.

FLUFFY BREAKFAST PANCAKES

Difficulty level: Easy

Preparation time: 10 minutes

Cooking time: 10 minutes

Servings: 5

Ingredients:

- 4 eggs
- 2 tbsp swerve
- 1 tbsp coconut oil
- ½ cup butter, melted
- 2 cups almond flour
- 1 tsp baking powder
- ½ tsp vanilla
- ¼ cup water
- 1 pinch of salt

Directions:

1. Add all ingredients into the blender and blend until well combined.
2. Preheat the griddle to medium heat.
3. Spray the griddle top with cooking spray.
4. Pour ⅓cup of pancake batter on the hot griddle top and cook until pancake edges are firm.
5. Flip to the other side and cook for a minute.
6. Serve and enjoy.

BROCCOLI HASH BROWNS

Difficulty level: Easy

Preparation time: 10 minutes

Cooking time: 15 minutes

Servings: 12

Ingredients:

- 1 egg
- 4 oz Cheddar cheese, shredded
- 3 cups broccoli rice
- ¼ tsp garlic powder
- ¼ tsp onion powder
- 3 cups cauliflower rice
- ¼ tsp pepper
- ¼ tsp salt

Directions:

1. Add broccoli rice and cauliflower rice to a microwave-safe bowl and microwave for 5 minutes. Squeeze out all excess liquid of broccoli and cauliflower rice.
2. Add vegetable rice to a bowl.
3. Add egg, garlic powder, onion powder, cheese, pepper, and salt and mix well to combine.
4. Preheat the griddle to medium heat.
5. Spray the griddle top with cooking spray.
6. Make patties from the mixture, place them on the hot griddle top and cook until lightly browned from both sides.
7. Serve and enjoy

CREAM CHEESE PANCAKES

Difficulty level: Medium

Preparation time: 5 minutes

Cooking time: 5 minutes

Servings: 2

Ingredients:

- 2 eggs
- 2 oz cream cheese
- ½ tsp cinnamon
- 1 tbsp Erythritol

Directions:

1. Add all ingredients into the blender and blend until smooth.
2. Preheat the griddle to medium heat.
3. Spray the griddle top with cooking spray.
4. Pour ¼ cup of batter on the hot griddle top and cook for 2 minutes.
5. Flip pancake and cook for 1 minute.
6. Serve and enjoy.

FLUFFY BLUEBERRY PANCAKES

Difficulty level: Medium

Preparation time: 10 minutes

Cooking time: 10 minutes

Servings: 4

Ingredients:

- 1cup flour
- ¾ cup milk
- 2 tbsp white vinegar
- 2 tbsp sugar
- 1 tsp baking powder
- ½ tsp baking soda
- ½ tsp salt
- 1 egg
- 2 tbsp butter, melted
- 1cup fresh blueberries

Directions:

1   In a bowl, combine the milk and vinegar. Set aside for 2 minutes.
2   In a large bowl, combine the flour, sugar, baking powder, baking soda, and salt. Stir in the milk, egg, blueberries, and melted butter. Mix until combined but not totally smooth.
3   Heat your griddle to medium heat and add a little butter.
4   Pour the pancakes onto the griddle and cook until one side is golden brown.

5   Flip the pancakes and cook until the other side is golden.

6   Remove the pancakes from the griddle and serve with warm maple syrup.

SIMPLE FRENCH CREPES

Difficulty level: Easy

Preparation time: 1 hour

Cooking time: 15 minutes

Servings: 4

Ingredients:

- 1 ¼cup flour
- ¾ cup whole milk
- ½ cup water
- 2 eggs
- 3 tbsp unsalted butter, melted
- 1 tbsp vanilla
- 2 tbsp sugar

Directions:

1   In a large bowl, add all the ingredients and mix with a whisk. Make sure the batter is smooth. Rest for 1 hour.

2   Heat your gas griddle to medium heat and add a thin layer of butter. Add about ¼ cup of the batter. Using a crepe-spreading tool, form your crepe and cook for 1–2 minutes. Use your crepe spatula and flip. Cook for another minute.

3   Top with Nutella and strawberries for a sweet crepe, or top with scrambled eggs and black forest ham for a savory crepe

MINI PORTOBELLO BURGERS

Difficulty level: Easy

Preparation time: 15 minutes

Cooking time: 15 minutes

Servings: 4

Ingredients:

- 2 Portobello mushroom caps
- 2 slices of Mozzarella cheese
- 4 buns, like brioche

For the marinade:

- ¼ cup balsamic vinegar
- 2 tbsp olive oil
- 1 tsp dried basil
- 1 tsp dried oregano
- 1 tsp garlic powder
- ¼ tsp sea salt
- ¼ tsp black pepper

Directions:

1   Whisk together the marinade ingredients in a large mixing bowl. Add mushroom caps and toss to coat.
2   Let stand at room temperature for 15 minutes, turning twice.
3   Preheat the griddle to medium-high heat.
4   Place mushrooms on the griddle; reserve marinade for basting.

5   Cook for 5–8 minutes on each side or until tender.

6   Brush with marinade frequently.

7   Top with Mozzarella cheese during the last 2 minutes of cooking.

8   Remove from griddle and serve on brioche buns.

HOMEMADE FRENCH CREPES

Difficulty level: Easy

Preparation time: 1 hour

Cooking time: 15 minutes

Servings: 4

Ingredients:

- 1 ¼ cup flour
- ¾ cup whole milk
- ½ cup water
- 2 eggs
- 3 tbsp unsalted butter, melted
- 1 tsp vanilla
- 2 tbsp sugar

Directions:

1   In a large bowl, add all the ingredients and mix with a whisk. Make sure the batter is smooth. Rest for 1 hour.

2   Heat your griddle to medium heat and add a thin layer of butter. Add about ¼ cup of the batter. Using a crepe-spreading tool, form your crepe and cook for 1–2 minutes. Use your crepe spatula and flip. Cook for another minute.

3   Top with Nutella and strawberries for a sweet crepe, scrambled eggs and black forest ham for a savory crepe.

GLUTEN-FREE SPICY EGG SCRAMBLED

Difficulty level: Easy

Preparation time: 10 minutes

Cooking time: 10 minutes

Servings: 2

Ingredients:

- 4 eggs
- 2 tbsp cilantro, chopped
- ⅓ cup heavy cream
- 1 tomato, diced
- 3 tbsp butter
- 1 Serrano chili pepper, chopped
- 2 tbsp scallions, sliced
- ¼ tsp pepper
- ½ tsp salt

Directions:

1 Preheat the griddle to medium heat.
2 Melt butter on top of the hot griddle.
3 Add tomato and chili pepper and sauté for 2 minutes.
4 Whisk eggs with cilantro, cream, pepper, and salt in a bowl.
5 Pour egg mixture over tomato and chili pepper and stir until egg is set.
6 Garnish with scallions and serve.

CHOCOLATE PANCAKE

Difficulty level: Medium

Preparation time: 10 minutes

Cooking time: 10 minutes

Servings: 4

Ingredients:

- 2 eggs
- ½ tsp baking powder
- 2 tbsp Erythritol
- 1 ½ tbsp cocoa powder
- ¼ cup ground flaxseed
- 2 tbsp water
- 1 tsp nutmeg
- 1 tsp cinnamon
- ¼ tsp salt

Directions:

1   In a bowl, mix ground flaxseed, baking powder, Erythritol, cocoa powder, spices, and salt.
2   Add eggs and stir well.
3   Add water and stir until the batter is well combined.
4   Preheat the griddle to medium-low heat.
5   Spray the griddle top with cooking spray.
6   Pour a large spoonful of batter on a hot griddle top and make a pancake.

7   Cook the pancake for 3–4 minutes on each side.

8   Serve and enjoy.

CLASSIC DENVER OMELET

Difficulty level: Easy

Preparation time: 5 minutes

Cooking time: 10 minutes

Servings: 4

Ingredients:

- 6 large eggs
- ¼ cup country ham, diced
- ¼ cup yellow onion, finely chopped
- ¼ cup green bell pepper, chopped
- ⅔ cup Cheddar cheese, shredded
- ¼ tsp cayenne pepper
- ¼ tsp salt and black pepper
- 2 tbsp butter

Directions:

1 Heat your griddle to medium heat and place the butter onto the griddle.
2 Add the ham, onion, and pepper to the butter and cook until the vegetables have just softened.
3 Beat the eggs in a large bowl and add a pinch of salt and the cayenne pepper.

4   Split the vegetables into two portions on the griddle and add half of the eggs to each portion. Cook until the eggs have begun to firm up, and then add the cheese to each omelet.

5   Fold the omelets over and remove them from the griddle. Serve immediately.

GRILLED BERRIES TOAST WITH CINNAMON

Difficulty level: Easy

Preparation time: 15 minutes

Cooking time: 10 minutes

Servings: 4

Ingredients:

- 1 (15oz) can of full-fat coconut milk, refrigerated overnight
- ½ tbsp powdered sugar
- 1 ½ tsp vanilla extract, divided
- 1 cup strawberries, halved
- 1 tbsp maple syrup, plus more for garnish
- 1 tbsp brown sugar, divided
- ¾ cup lite coconut milk
- 2 large eggs
- ½ tsp ground cinnamon
- 2 tbsp butter, unsalted and at room temperature
- 4 slices of challah bread

Directions:

1 Turn the chilled can of full-fat coconut milk upside down (do not shake the can), open the bottom, then pour out the liquid coconut water. Scoop the remaining solid coconut cream into a medium bowl. Wash the cream for 3–5 minutes using an electric hand mixer until soft peaks form.

2 Add the powdered sugar and ½ tsp the vanilla to the coconut cream, and whip it again until creamy. Put the bowl in the refrigerator.

3   Preheat the griddle to medium-high. While the unit is preheating, mix the strawberries with the maple syrup and toss to coat evenly.

4   Sprinkle evenly using ½ tbsp brown sugar.

5   Whisk together the lite coconut milk, eggs, the remaining 1 tsp vanilla, and cinnamon using a large shallow bowl.

6   Put the strawberries on the grill top. Gently press the fruit down to maximize grill marks. Then, grill for 4 minutes without flipping.

7   Meanwhile, butter each slice of bread on both sides. Put one slice in the egg mixture and let it soak for 1 minute. Flip the slice over and soak it for another minute. Repeat for the remaining bread slices. Sprinkle each side of the toast using the remaining ½ tbsp brown sugar.

8   After 4 minutes, remove the strawberries from the grill and set them aside. Decrease the temperature to medium-low. Put the bread on the grill and cook for 4–6 minutes, until golden and caramelized. Check often to achieve the desired doneness.

9   Put the toast on a plate and top using the strawberries and whipped coconut cream.

10 Drizzle with maple syrup, if desired.

SALMON BURGERS

Difficulty level: Easy

Preparation time: 10 minutes

Cooking time: 15 minutes

Servings: 4

Ingredients:
- 2 potato buns
- 2 lb salmon, finely chopped
- ½ red onion, finely chopped
- 1 stalk celery, finely chopped
- ½ tsp garlic powder
- 1 tsp Dijon mustard
- 1 tsp salt
- 2 slices tomato
- 1 tbsp vegetable oil

Directios:

1 Combine the chopped salmon, onion, celery, garlic powder, mustard, and salt in a large bowl. Mix well and form into 4 equal patties.
2 Heat your griddle to medium heat and add the vegetable oil. When the oil is shimmering, add the salmon patties, cooking for 6–7 minutes per side. Remove from the griddle, place on the buns, and top with sliced tomato to serve.

GLUTEN-FREE OATMEAL PANCAKES

Difficulty level: Easy

Preparation time: 15 minutes **Cooking time:** 5 minutes

Servings: 8

Ingredients:

- ¾ cup old-fashioned oats
- ¾ cup oat flour
- 1 tsp baking powder
- ½ tsp salt
- 1 egg
- 1 cup milk
- 2 tbsp vegetable oil
- 4 tbsp honey

Directions:

1. Preheat the outdoor gas griddle to medium heat.
2. Mix the oats, oat flour, brown sugar, baking powder, baking soda, spices, and salt in a bowl.
3. Add egg, milk, and oil in a second bowl and beat until well combined.
4. Add the flour mixture to the bowl of egg mixture and mix until just moistened.
5. Grease the griddle lightly.
6. Place about ¼ cup of the mixture onto the griddle and spread in an even layer.
7. Repeat with the remaining mixture.
8. Cook each pancake for about 2–3 minutes or until golden brown.

9. Carefully flip the pancakes and cook for about 1–2 minutes or until golden brown.

10. Serve warm with the drizzling of honey.

POTATO PANCAKES

Difficulty level: Medium

Preparation time: 15 minutes **Cooking time:** 4 minutes

Servings: 8

Ingredients:

- ¼ cup milk
- 2 eggs
- 1½ cup potato, shredded
- ¼ cup flour
- ¼ cup onion, chopped finely
- ¼ cup scallion, chopped finely
- 1 tsp baking powder
- 1 tsp salt
- 1 tsp ground black pepper

Directions:

1   In a bowl, beat together the milk and eggs until frothy.
2   Add in the potato and remaining ingredients and stir to combine.
3   Set the potato mixture aside for about 20 minutes.
4   Preheat the outdoor gas griddle to medium-high heat.
5   Grease the griddle lightly.
6   Place about ¼ cup of the mixture onto the griddle and spread in an even layer.
7   Repeat with the remaining mixture.
8   Cook each pancake for about 2–3 minutes or until golden brown.

9   Carefully flip the pancakes and cook for about 1½ – 2 minutes or until golden brown.

10 Serve warm.

BROCCOLI PANCAKES

Difficulty level: Easy

Preparation time: 15 minutes

Cooking time: 5 minutes

Servings: 4

Ingredients:

- 1 cup broccoli florets
- 1 small onion, chopped roughly
- 1 garlic clove, peeled
- 1 egg
- ½ cup whole milk
- 1 cup all-purpose flour
- 1 tsp baking powder
- 5 fresh chives, chopped
- 1 tbsp fresh chervil, chopped
- Salt and ground black pepper, to taste

Directions:

1. Preheat the outdoor gas griddle to medium-high heat.
2. Add the broccoli, onion, and garlic into a blender and pulse until finely chopped.
3. Add the egg, milk, flour, and baking powder and pulse on medium speed until a thick mixture forms.
4. Transfer the broccoli mixture to a bowl.
5. Add the chives, chervil, salt, and black pepper and stir to combine.

6   Grease the griddle lightly.

7   Place about 2 tbsp of the mixture onto the griddle and spread in an even layer.

8   Repeat with the remaining mixture.

9   Cook the pancakes for about 3 minutes or until golden brown.

10 Carefully flip the pancakes and cook for about 2 minutes or until golden brown.

11 Serve warm

MEAT RECIPES

SIZZLING CHICKEN FAJITAS

Difficulty level: Medium

Cooking temperature: 400°F

Preparation time: 5 minutes

Cooking time: 25 minutes

Servings: 4

Ingredients:

- 4 boneless chicken breast halves, thinly sliced
- 1 yellow onion, sliced
- 1 large green bell pepper, sliced
- 1 large red bell pepper, sliced
- 1 tsp ground cumin
- 1 tsp garlic powder
- 1 tsp onion powder
- 2 tbsp lime juice
- 1 tbsp olive oil
- ½ tsp black pepper
- 1 tsp salt
- 3 tbsp vegetable oil
- 10 flour tortillas

Directions:

1 In a zipper-lock bag, combine the chicken, cumin, garlic, onion, lime juice, salt, pepper, and olive oil. Allow marinating for 30 minutes.
2 Preheat the griddle to medium heat.

3   Add olive oil on one side of the griddle and heat until shimmering. Add the onion and pepper and cook until slightly softened.

4   On the other side of the griddle, add the marinated chicken and cook until lightly browned.

5   Once the chicken is lightly browned, toss with the onion and pepper and cook until the chicken registers 165°F.

6   Remove chicken and vegetables from the griddle and serve with warm tortillas.

MARINATED LAMB CHOPS WITH GRILLED POLENTA STICKS

Difficulty level: Easy

Cooking temperature: 280°F

Preparation time: 10 minutes

Cooking time: 7 minutes

Servings: 2

Ingredients:

- 6 lamb chops
- ½ cup olive oil
- ½ cup red wine vinegar
- 6–8 fresh garlic cloves, peeled & roughly chopped
- 2 tsp oregano, dried
- Salt, as needed
- Pepper, as needed
- Butter, as needed
- Grilled polenta sticks

Directions :

1   Pour the olive oil and red wine vinegar on the lamb chops. Mix the garlic, oregano, salt, and pepper, then rub it all over the chops until well-coated. Let it marinate for 15–20 minutes at room temperature before cooking.

2   Warm your gas griddle to high heat. Spread the butter on your griddle, then add the lamb chops. Sear for 3–4 minutes per side.

3   Flip the lamb chops to the other side, adding more butter if required. Adjust to medium low heat to finish cooking. Let it rest on a serving dish with 1 tbsp butter spread out on the dish.

4   Serve with grilled polenta sticks and enjoy!

GARLIC-ROSEMARY LEG OF LAMB

Difficulty level: Medium

Cooking temperature: 320°F

Preparation time: 10 minutes

Cooking time: 8 minutes

Servings: 4

Ingredients:

- 1 (2–3 lb) leg of lamb, boneless
- ⅛ cup olive oil
- 4 large garlic cloves, smashed & chopped
- 1 tbsp rosemary, minced
- Salt, as needed
- Freshly ground pepper, as needed

Directions :

1   Put the lamb on your work surface, then slice between the muscles using a paring knife to separate them. Remove any excess fat from the lamb.
2   Mix the olive oil, garlic, and rosemary in a large shallow dish. Add the lamb, coat it evenly, and let it marinate for 4 hours at room temperature, flipping it several times.
3   Warm your gas grill to medium-high heat. Flavor the lamb with salt and pepper, then grill it on medium-high heat, flipping it often, for 8 minutes, until evenly cooked.

4 Transfer the cooked leg of lamb to your carving board, wrap it loosely
with foil, and let it rest for 15 minutes before slicing. Serve.

58

LAMB CHOPS WITH KEFIR VERDE SAUCE

Difficulty level: Hard

Cooking temperature: 320°F

Preparation time: 10 minutes

Cooking time: 12 minutes

Servings: 2

Ingredients :

For the lamb:

- 8 lamb chops
- 1 tsp ground black pepper
- 2 tbsp sea salt
- 3 garlic cloves, minced
- ½ cup fresh mint, chopped
- 1 ½ cup fresh pomegranate juice

For the kefir salsa verde:

- 2 bunches of green onions, whole
- 2 tbsp olive oil
- ½ tbsp sea salt
- 1 garlic clove, peeled
- 1 cup fresh parsley, chopped
- 1 cup organic plain whole-milk kefir

Directions:

<u>For the lamb:</u>

1   Mix the black pepper, sea salt, garlic, mint, and pomegranate juice in a large bowl. Add the lamb, mix it well to coat evenly, and keep it in your refrigerator overnight to marinate. Remove the marinated lamb 1 hour before cooking, then remove excess marinade from the lamb. Warm your gas grill to high heat.
2   Brush the grill grates using oil, then grill the lamb chops on high heat for 5 minutes per side. Set aside 10 minutes to rest.

<u>For the salsa verde:</u>

1   Coat the green onions with olive oil and sea salt in a medium bowl, then cook them on your gas grill until blackened. Set aside to cool.
2   Add the blackened green onions, garlic, parsley, and kefir in your blender, then purée until smooth, serve the lamb chops on your large serving plate with the salsa verde on the side. Enjoy!

GLUTEN-FREE TURKISH LAMB KEBABS

Difficulty level: Easy

Cooking temperature: 340°F

Preparation time: 10 minutes

Cooking time: 8 minutes

Servings: 4

Ingredients:

For the kebabs:

- 1¾ lb ground lamb
- Flatbread, for serving
- 1 red onion, sliced
- Greek yogurt, as needed

For the marinade:

- 3 garlic cloves, minced
- 3 tbsp olive oil
- 1 tbsp tomato paste
- ½ tsp paprika
- ¼ tsp cayenne pepper
- ¼ tsp ground cinnamon
- ¼ tsp ground cumin
- 2 tbsp fresh thyme leaves
- Sea salt, as needed

- Finely ground black pepper, as needed

Directions:

1   Mix all the marinade ingredients in a bowl until well combined. Add the lamb meat to it and toss to coat evenly. Let it marinate for 2 hours at room temperature. Warm your gas grill to high heat, thread the lamb onto skewers, and grill them for 3–4 minutes per side on high heat or until done to your liking.
2   Remove the cooked lamb kebabs off your skewers, transfer them to your flatbread (if desired), then serve with red onion slices and Greek yogurt on the side.

MARINATED PORK CHOPS

Difficulty level: Medium

Cooking temperature: 300°F

Preparation time: 10 minutes

Cooking time: 10 minutes

Servings: 4

Ingredients:

- 4 pork chops
- ¼ tsp cayenne
- ½ tsp pepper
- 1 tsp garlic, minced
- 2 tbsp olive oil
- ¼ cup soy sauce
- ⅓ cup Worcestershire sauce
- ⅓ cup balsamic vinegar
- 1 tsp salt

Directions:

1. Add pork chops and remaining ingredients into the Ziplock bag. Seal the bag, shake well, and place in the refrigerator for 4 hours.
2. Preheat the griddle to medium heat.
3. Spray the griddle top with cooking spray.

4. Place marinated pork chops on a hot griddle top and cook for 3–5 minutes on each side or until internal temperature reaches 145°F.

5. Serve and enjoy.

PORK TENDERLOIN IN BOURBON

Difficulty level: Hard

Cooking temperature: 100°F

Preparation time: 24 hours

Cooking time: 1 hour

Servings: 10

Ingredients:

- 2 cups white sugar
- ½ cup Jim Beam® Bourbon
- 2 cups water
- 2 tsp vanilla extract
- 3–4 lb pork tenderloin
- 2 tsp black pepper
- 2 tsp garlic powder
- 2 tbsp salt

Directions:

1. In a medium bowl, combine sugar, Jim Beam® Bourbon, water, salt, and vanilla. Mix well. Place tenderloin in a large zip bag and pour ½ of the marinade over the top. Refrigerate for 24 hours. Season tenderloin with garlic and pepper.
2. Heat your griddle for two-zone griddling and brush the rack with vegetable oil.
3. Remove to a cutting board and slice against the grain.

HOT PORK SANDWICHES

Difficulty level: Easy

Cooking temperature: 100°F

Preparation time: 24 hours

Cooking time: 12 hours

Servings: 30

Ingredients:

- 1 boneless pork butt (5–6lb)
- 2 tbsp smoked paprika
- 2 tbsp hickory salt
- 1 tbsp black pepper
- 2 cups cider vinegar
- 1 cup Southern Comfort
- 1 cup water
- 2 tbsp molasses
- 2 tbsp salt
- ¼ cup hot sauce
- 1 tbsp red pepper flakes
- 1 tbsp black pepper
- 2 tsp ground cayenne

Directions:

1   In a bowl, combine paprika, hickory salt, 1 tbsp black pepper, and cayenne. Coat pork shoulder with seasonings and cover with plastic wrap. Refrigerate for 24 hours.

2   Preheat the griddle to medium heat. Place pork shoulder on griddle and smoke. Place a thermometer on the grate to track the temperature. Combine remaining ingredients for basting.

3   Remove from heat and allow to rest 20 minutes (still in foil) and then unwrap and rest another 10 minutes. Shred pork, tossing with reserved pan juices.

4   Serve on soft white rolls, topped with your favorite coleslaw.

PORK PATTIES

Difficulty level: Hard

Cooking temperature: 300°F

Preparation time: 10 minutes

Cooking time: 30 minutes

Servings: 2

Ingredients:

- ½ tsp salt
- ¾ tsp ground sage
- ⅛ tsp ground nutmeg
- ½ tsp onion powder
- ⅛ tsp red pepper
- ¾ tsp fennel seeds
- ½ tsp dried thyme
- 1 tsp garlic powder
- ¾ tsp pepper
- 1 lb ground pork

Directions:

1. Turn on the griddle to preheat.
2. Mix all the ingredients and prepare 8 patties from the mixture.
3. Grease the griddle with cooking oil.
4. Arrange patties on the griddle and cook for 5 minutes per side.
5. Transfer to a plate and serve.

PORK PINEAPPLE SKEWERS

Difficulty level: Easy

Cooking temperature: 300°F

Preparation time: 10 minutes

Cooking time: 20 minutes

Servings: 2

Ingredients:

- 2 tbsp creole seasoning
- 1 tbsp hot sauce
- 2 cups pineapple cubes
- 1 tsp ground allspice
- 1 lime juice
- 1 lb pork fillet

Directions:

1   Allow the griddle to preheat.
2   Mix all the ingredients.
3   Grease the griddle with cooking oil.
4   String pork and pineapple chunks onto skewers.
5   Arrange them on the griddle and cook for a few minutes on each side.
6   Serve and enjoy!

SWEET SMOKED PORK RIBS

Difficulty level: Easy

Cooking temperature: 300°F

Preparation time: 10 minutes

Cooking time: 40 minutes

Servings: 2

Ingredients:

- 10 lb baby back pork ribs

For the rub:

- 1 tbsp cumin
- 1 tbsp chili powder
- 2 tbsp onion powder
- 2 tbsp packed brown sugar
- 1 tbsp smoked paprika
- 1 tbsp garlic powder
- 2 tbsp ground white pepper
- 1 tsp liquid smoke

For the sauce:

- ¼ cup barbeque sauce
- ¼ cup packed brown sugar
- 1 cup apple juice

Directions:

1 Take a bowl and all the ingredients to rub in it. Mix well.

2 Take baby back pork ribs and coat them with the rub.

3 Marinate in the fridge after transferring them to a plastic bag.

4 Allow the griddle to preheat; when hot, add the ribs.

5 Cook them for 40 minutes.

6 Prepare the sauce by cooking the ingredients in a saucepan until it thickens, then pour it over the ribs.

7 Cook them for additional 20 minutes.

8 Serve and enjoy!

HAM AND CHEESE SANDWICH

Difficulty level: Medium

Cooking temperature: 370°F

Preparation time: 10 minutes

Cooking time: 15 minutes

Servings: 4

Ingredients:

- 16 sweet ham, thin slices
- 2 cups Gruyère cheese, shredded
- ½ stick butter, unsalted
- 2 tbsp bacon fat
- ¼ cup all-purpose flour
- 1 ½ cup whole milk
- 8 crusty white bread, slices
- ¼ cup spicy brown mustard
- Olive oil, as needed
- Salt, as needed
- Pepper, as needed

Directions:

1 Warm your gas griddle to medium heat, add a small cast iron sauce pot, and add the butter and bacon fat. Spread until melted. Add the flour, then stir to combine well. Cook for 3–4 minutes, then pour ⅓

cup of the milk, stirring continuously. Pour the rest of the milk and whisk again to combine.

2   Cook for 5–7 minutes more on low heat. Add salt and pepper to taste and ⅓ of the gruyère, then stir until melted. Toast the bread on all sides with some olive oil. Thinly spread the mustard on each bread slice, then add some gruyère on top. Put 2 slices of ham on the cheese, then some creamy sauce.

3   Add 2 more ham pieces and more gruyère on top. Put one slice of bread on top to make the sandwich, then put on your gas griddle on low heat until the cheese melts. Enjoy!

BUFFALO CHICKEN RANCH BURGER

Difficulty level: Hard

Cooking temperature: 380°F

Preparation time: 10 minutes

Cooking time: 5 minutes

Servings: 2

Ingredients:

- 2 large chicken breasts, chopped
- ½ cup wing sauce
- ¼ cup ranch dressing
- 1 tsp garlic powder
- 1 tsp parsley, dried
- Salt, as needed
- Pepper, as needed
- 1 tbsp oil
- ¼ lb American cheese, deli thin-sliced
- Arugula salad, as needed
- 2 Burger buns

Directions:

1 Warm your gas griddle to medium-high heat, then grease it with oil. Add the chicken, then stir to cook for 3–4 minutes until evenly cooked; adjust the heat to medium, then season the chicken with salt,

pepper, garlic, and parsley. Pour the wing sauce and mix until evenly coated. Add more if you like.

2   Mix in the ranch dressing and then add about 6 slices of cheese. Melt throughout your chicken, adjust heat to medium-low, split your chicken into 2 piles, put a couple of extra slices of cheese over each pile, and put the rolls over the cheese for 30–60 seconds.

3   Put your hands on the buns and flip using the spatula under the sandwich. Serve and enjoy!

PINEAPPLE BEEF BURGER PATTIES

Difficulty level: Easy

Cooking temperature: 390°F

Preparation time: 10 minutes

Cooking time: 20 minutes

Servings: 4

Ingredients:

- ¼ lb beef
- 2 slices pineapple
- ¼ tsp pepper
- 1 tsp ginger
- ¼ cup soy sauce
- ¼ cup green onions
- 1 garlic clove
- Salt to taste

Directions:

1. Take a bowl, add all ingredients to it and mix them well.
2. Prepare the griddle, preheat it to high temperature, and brush its surface with olive oil.
3. Take the mixture, place the patties on a griddle, and cook for 4–5 minutes on each side.
4. Finally, serve and enjoy it

CAPRESE STEAK

Difficulty level: Hard

Cooking temperature: 400°F

Preparation time: 10 minutes

Cooking time: 30 minutes

Servings: 4

Ingredients:

- 2 tomatoes
- 4 oz fresh Mozzarella
- 6 oz flank steaks
- 8 basil leaves
- Salt & Pepper to taste
- 3 tbsp Olive oil
- 3 tbsp Balsamic vinegar

Directions:

1 Take fillets to brush them with olive oil and season them with pepper and salt.
2 Prepare the griddle, preheat it to high temperature, and brush its surface with olive oil
3 Place the steak on the griddle, cook for 5 minutes, flip the side, and again cook for 5 more minutes, then add the slice of Mozzarella on top.
4 Remove from the griddle and top with basil leaves & tomato slices.
5 Finally, serve and enjoy it!

CAJUN MOJO STEAK KEBABS

Difficulty level: Easy

Cooking temperature: 390°F

Preparation time: 10 minutes

Cooking time: 5 minutes

Servings: 4

Ingredients:

- 2 lb New York strip steak, sliced into 2-inch cubes
- 2 tbsp Steak Dry Rub
- 1 cup orange juice
- ¼ cup tequila
- 2 tbsp Cajun Spice Rub
- ¼ cup lime juice
- 2 tbsp Mojo Marinade
- Wooden skewers, as needed

Directions:

1   Add the steak, Steak Dry Rub, orange juice, lime juice, a bit of olive oil, and Cajun Spice Rub in a large bowl, then mix evenly and put in your fridge for 30–45 minutes; remove the meat, then thread the steak cubes on your wooden skewers.

2   Warm your gas griddle to medium-high heat, cook the kebabs for 2 minutes, drizzle a bit of Mojo Marinade on top, and flip to cook evenly. Transfer the skewers to a large serving plate and drizzle some Mojo Marinade on top. Serve and enjoy!

CHIPOTLE ADOBE CHICKEN

Difficulty level: Hard

Cooking temperature: 100°F

Preparation time: 1 – 24 hours

Cooking time: 20 minutes

Servings: 4

Ingredients:

- 2 lb chicken thighs or breasts (boneless, skinless)

For the marinade:

- ¼ cup olive oil
- 2 chipotle peppers in adobo sauce, plus 1 tsp adobo sauce from the can
- 1 tbsp garlic, minced
- 1 shallot, finely chopped
- 1 ½ tbsp cumin
- 1 tbsp cilantro, super-finely chopped or dried
- 2 tsp chili powder
- 1 tsp dried oregano
- ½ tsp salt
- 1 tbsp fresh limes, garnish
- 1 tbsp cilantro, garnish

Directions:

1. Preheat griddle to medium-high.
2. Add marinade ingredients to a food processor or blender and pulse into a paste.
3. Add the chicken and marinade to a sealable plastic bag and massage to coat well.
4. Place in the refrigerator for 1 hour to 24 hours before cooking.
5. Sear chicken for 7 minutes, turn and cook an additional 7 minutes.
6. Turn heat to low and continue to cook until the chicken has reached an internal temperature of 165°F.
7. Remove chicken from griddle and allow to rest 5–10 minutes before serving.
8. Garnish with a squeeze of fresh lime and a sprinkle of cilantro to serve.

ULTIMATE GRIDDLE CHEESEBURGER

Difficulty level: Hard

Cooking temperature: 390°F

Preparation time: 10 minutes

Cooking time: 40 minutes

Servings: 4

Ingredients:

- 2 buns
- 3 tbsp butter
- 1 slice provolone cheese
- 3 tbsp mayonnaise
- 1 slice of yellow American cheese
- 4 slices tomato
- 4 slices of Cheddar cheese

Directions:

1   Preheat the griddle.
2   Apply the butter and mayonnaise to the buns.
3   Sauté the bun on the griddle and put the remaining ingredients over it.
4   Cover with a second bun and sauté on the griddle again.
5   Serve and enjoy.

CAPRESE BASIL FLANK STEAK

Difficulty level: Medium

Cooking temperature: 370°F

Preparation time: 10 minutes

Cooking time: 10 minutes

Servings: 4

Ingredients:

- (6 oz) flank steaks
- 1 tbsp sea salt, for seasoning
- 1 tbsp flakey sea salt, for serving
- 1 tbsp fresh ground pepper
- 1 tbsp olive oil
- 2 Roma tomatoes, sliced
- 1 oz fresh buffalo mozzarella, cut into four slices
- 8 fresh basil leaves
- 1 tbsp balsamic vinegar glaze for drizzling

Directions:

1. Lightly brush each filet, on all sides, with olive oil and season with salt and pepper.
2. Preheat the griddle to high. Place steaks on the griddle, reduce heat to medium, tent with foil, and cook for 5 minutes. Flip, re-tent, and cook for an additional 5 minutes; during the last 2 minutes of cooking, top each with a slice of Mozzarella.

3. Remove steaks from the griddle and top each with a few tomato slices
    and basil leaves. Drizzle with balsamic glaze, and sprinkle with flakey
    salt and a little more black peppers.

GLUTEN-FREE DIJON BEEF BURGER PATTIES

Difficulty level: Easy

Cooking temperature: 390°F

Preparation time: 10 minutes

Cooking time: 20 minutes

Servings: 4

Ingredients:

- 1 lb beef
- ½ tsp salt
- ¾ tbsp Worcestershire sauce
- ½ tsp pepper
- ⅛ tsp cayenne
- 1 tbsp Dijon mustard
- ⅛ tsp chili flakes
- 1 tbsp parsley

Directions:

1. Take a bowl, add all ingredients to it and mix them well.
2. Prepare the griddle, preheat it to high temperature, and brush its surface with olive oil.
3. Make the patties from the mixture, place them on the griddle and cook for 5–8 minutes on each side.
4. Finally, serve and enjoy it!

HAWAIIAN CHICKEN SKEWERS

Difficulty level: Hard

Cooking temperature: 120°F

Preparation time: 1 hour 10 minutes

Cooking time: 15 minutes

Servings: 4

Ingredients:

- 1 lb boneless, skinless chicken breast cut into 1½-inch cubes
- 3 cups pineapple, cut into 1 ½-inch cubes
- 2 large green peppers, cut into 1 ½-inch pieces
- 1 large red onion, cut into 1 ½-inch pieces
- 2 tbsp olive oil to coat veggies

For the marinade:

- ⅓ cup tomato paste
- ⅓ cup brown sugar, packed
- ⅓ cup soy sauce
- ¼ cup pineapple juice
- 2 tbsp olive oil
- 1 ½ tbsp mirin or rice wine vinegar
- 4 tsp garlic cloves, minced
- 1 tbsp ginger, minced
- ½ tsp sesame oil
- 1 tbsp sea salt

- 1 tbsp ground black pepper

- 10 wooden skewers for assembly

Directions:

1 Combine marinade ingredients in a mixing bowl until smooth. Reserve ½ cup of the marinade in the refrigerator.

2 Add chicken and remaining marinade to a sealable plastic bag and refrigerate for 1 hour.

3 Soak 10 wooden skewer sticks in water for 1 hour.

4 Preheat the griddle to medium heat.

5 Add red onion, bell pepper, and pineapple to a mixing bowl with 2 tbsp olive oil and toss to coat.

6 Thread red onion, bell pepper, pineapple, and chicken onto the skewers until all the chicken has been used.

7 Place the skewers on the griddle and grab your reserved marinade from the refrigerator; cook for 5 minutes, then brush with the remaining marinade and rotate.

8 Brush again with marinade and sear for about 5 additional minutes or until chicken reads 165°F on a meat thermometer.

9 Serve warm.

CHICKEN THIGHS WITH GINGER-SESAME GLAZE

Difficulty level: Medium

Cooking temperature: 120°F

Preparation time: 10 minutes

Cooking time: 20 minutes

Servings: 4

Ingredients:

- 8 boneless, skinless chicken thighs

For the glaze:

- 3 tbsp dark brown sugar
- 2 ½ tbsp soy sauce
- 1 tbsp fresh garlic, minced
- 2 tsp sesame seeds
- 1 tsp fresh ginger, minced
- 1 tsp Sambal Oelek
- ⅓ cup scallions, thinly sliced
- 1 tbsp nonstick cooking spray

Directions:

1. Combine glaze ingredients in a large mixing bowl; separate and reserve half for serving.
2. Add chicken to bowl and toss to coat well.

3. Preheat the griddle to medium-high heat.

4. Coat with cooking spray.

5. Cook chicken for 6 minutes on each side or until done.

6. Transfer chicken to plates and drizzle with remaining glaze to serve.

DIJON SALMON BURGERS

Difficulty level: Medium

Cooking temperature: 390°F

Preparation time: 2 hours

Cooking time: 11 minutes

Servings: 4

Ingredients:

- 1½ lb salmon fillet, skin and any remaining pin bones removed, cut into chunks
- 2 tsp Dijon mustard
- 3 scallions, trimmed and chopped
- ¼ cup bread crumbs (preferably fresh)
- 1 tbsp salt and pepper
- 1 tbsp good-quality olive oil for brushing
- 1tbsp sesame hamburger buns or 8–10 slider buns (like potato or dinner rolls)
- 1 large tomato, cut into 4 thick slices

Directions:

1. Put about one-quarter of the salmon and the mustard in a food processor and purée into a paste. Add the rest of the salmon and pulse until chopped. Transfer to a bowl, and add the scallions, bread crumbs, and a sprinkle of salt and pepper. Mix gently just enough to combine. Form into 4 burgers ¾–1-inch thick. Transfer to a plate and

cover with plastic wrap. Let them chill until firm (at least 2 or up to 8 hours).

2. Turn the control knob to the high position, when the griddle is hot, brush the burgers with oil on both sides, and then put them on the griddle. Cook for 11 minutes.

3. After 11 mins., check the burgers for doneness. Cooking is complete when the internal temperature reaches at least 165°F on a food thermometer. If necessary, close the hood and continue cooking for up to 2 minutes more.

4. Remove the burgers from the griddle. Put the buns on the griddle, cut side down, and toast for 1–2 minutes. Serve the burgers on the buns, topped with the tomato if used.

SUNDRIED TOMATO AND CHICKEN BURGER

Difficulty level: Hard

Cooking temperature: 390°F

Preparation time: 10 minutes

Cooking time: 60 minutes

Servings: 4

Ingredients:

- 4 buns
- 1 tbsp olive oil
- ½ cup grilled chicken
- 1 tsp red pepper flakes
- ½ cup tomatoes
- 1 tsp black pepper
- 6 fresh basil
- 1 tsp salt
- 3 cups Mozzarella cheese

Directions:

1   Preheat the griddle to high.
2   Take a bowl and mix in all the ingredients.
3   Sauté the mixture on the griddle.
4   Now place the buns on the surface board and fill them with a cooked mixture.
5   Serve and enjoy.

JUICY BEEF BURGER PATTIES

Difficulty level: Easy

Cooking temperature: 370°F

Preparation time: 10 minutes

Cooking time: 20 minutes

Servings: 4

Ingredients:

- 2 tbsp Worcestershire sauce
- 2 lb beef
- ¾ cup onion
- ½ tsp salt
- ½ tsp pepper

Directions:

1 Take a bowl, add all ingredients to it and mix them well.
2 Prepare the griddle, preheat it to high temperature, and brush its surface with olive oil.
3 Make the patties from the mixture and place them on the griddle and cook for 5–6 minutes from each side.
4 Finally, serve and enjoy it!

SPICY CAJUN PORK CHOPS

Difficulty level: Easy

Cooking temperature: 390°F

Preparation time: 10 minutes

Cooking time: 15 minutes

Servings: 4

Ingredients:

- 4 pork chops
- 1 tbsp paprika
- ½ tsp ground cumin
- ½ tsp dried sage
- ½ tsp salt
- ½ tsp black pepper
- ½ tsp garlic powder
- ¼ tsp cayenne pepper
- 1 tbsp butter
- 1 tbsp vegetable oil

Directions:

1. In a medium bowl, combine the paprika, cumin, sage, salt, pepper, garlic, and cayenne pepper.
2. Heat your griddle to medium-high heat and add the butter and oil.
3. Rub the pork chops with a generous amount of the seasoning rub.

4. Place the chops on the griddle and cook for 4–5 minutes. Turn the pork chops and continue cooking for an additional 4 minutes.

5. Remove the pork chops from the griddle and allow to rest for 5 minutes before serving.

GARLIC SOY PORK CHOPS

Difficulty level: Easy

Cooking temperature: 390°F

Preparation time: 10 minutes

Cooking time: 40 minutes

Servings: 2

Ingredients:

- ¼ cup butter
- ½ tsp salt
- ½ cup soy sauce
- 4 garlic cloves
- ½ tsp black pepper
- ½ tsp garlic powder
- ½ cup olive oil
- 6 pork chops

Directions:

1 Add garlic, soy sauce, garlic powder, pork chops, and olive oil to a plastic bag.
2 Put the bag in the refrigerator for half-hour to marinate.
3 Allow the griddle to preheat at medium heat.
4 Grease the griddle with olive oil and butter, then add the chops.
5 Cook for four minutes on each side.
6 Serve and enjoy!

ASIAN PORK SKEWERS

Difficulty level: Easy

Cooking temperature: 370°F

Preparation time: 10 minutes

Cooking time: 8 minutes

Servings: 12 Ingredients:

Ingredients:

* 1 ½lb pork tenderloin, cut into 1-inch pieces

For the marinade:

* ¾ tsp cornstarch
* ¼ tsp cayenne
* ½ tsp pepper
* 2 tsp five-spice powder
* ½ cup hoisin sauce
* ¼ tsp kosher salt

Directions:

1. Add pork pieces and marinade ingredients into the mixing bowl and mix well and let it marinate for 30 minutes.
2. Preheat the griddle to high heat.
3. Spray the griddle top with cooking spray.
4. Thread marinated pork pieces onto the skewers.

5. Place skewers on a hot griddle top and cook for 3–4 minutes on each side.
6. Serve and enjoy.

TURKEY BURGER PATTIES

Difficulty level: Medium

Cooking temperature: 390°F

Preparation time: 10 minutes

Cooking time: 10 minutes

Servings: 4

Ingredients:

- 1 lb ground turkey
- 1 tbsp garlic powder
- 1 ½ tbsp dried parsley
- 3 oz onion, diced
- 1 tbsp pepper
- 1 tbsp salt

Directions:

1. Add all ingredients into the bowl and mix until well combined.
2. Preheat the griddle to high heat.
3. Spray the griddle top with cooking spray.
4. Make patties from mixture and place on hot griddle top and cook for 5 minutes on each side.
5. Serve and enjoy.

GLUTEN-FREE SPINACH TURKEY PATTIES

Difficulty level: Easy

Cooking temperature: 390°F

Preparation time: 10 minutes

Cooking time: 10 minutes

Servings: 12 Ingredients:

Ingredients:

- 3 lb ground turkey
- 3 tbsp garlic, minced
- 1 onion, chopped
- 5 cups spinach, sautéed
- 3 tbsp mustard
- 1 tbsp pepper
- 1 tbsp salt

Directions:

1   Add all ingredients into the bowl and mix until well combined.
2   Preheat the griddle to high heat.
3   Spray the griddle top with cooking spray.
4   Make patties from mixture and place on hot griddle top and cook for 5 minutes on each side.
5   Serve and enjoy.

CREOLE CHICKEN STUFFED WITH CHEESE AND PEPPERS

Difficulty level: Easy

Cooking temperature: 370°F

Preparation time: 10 minutes

Cooking time: 20 minutes

Servings: 4

Ingredients:

- 4 boneless, skinless chicken breasts
- 8 mini sweet peppers, sliced thin and seeded
- 2 slices of Pepper Jack cheese, cut in half
- 2 slices of Colby Jack cheese, cut in half
- 1 tbsp creole seasoning, like Emeril's
- 1 tsp black pepper
- 1 tsp garlic powder
- 1 tsp onion powder
- 4 tsp olive oil, separated Toothpicks

Directions:

1 Rinse chicken and pat dry.
2 Mix creole seasoning, pepper, garlic powder, and onion powder together in a small mixing bowl and set aside.
3 Cut a slit on the side of each chicken breast; be careful not to cut through the chicken.
4 Rub each breast with 1 tsp of olive oil.

5   Rub each chicken breast with seasoning mix and coat evenly.

6   Stuff each breast of chicken with 1 half Pepper Jack cheese slice, 1 half Colby cheese slice, and a handful of pepper slices.

7   Secure the chicken shut with 4–5 toothpicks.

8   Preheat the griddle to medium-high and cook chicken for 8 minutes per side; or until chicken reaches an internal temperature of 165°F.

9   Allow chicken to rest for 5 minutes, remove toothpicks, and serve.

JUICY NY STRIP STEAK GRIDDLE

Difficulty level: Easy

Cooking temperature: 370°F

Preparation time: 45 minutes

Cooking time: 8 minutes

Servings: 1

Ingredients:

- 1 (8 oz) NY strip steak
- 1 tbsp olive oil
- 1 tbsp sea salt
- 1 tbsp fresh ground black pepper

Directions:

1. Putt off the steak from the fridge and let it come to room temperature, about 30–45 minutes.
2. Preheat the griddle to medium-high heat and brush with olive oil, season the steak on all sides with salt and pepper. Cook the steak for about 4–5 minutes.
3. Flip and cook about 4 minutes more for medium rare steak; between 125°F and 130°F on a meat thermometer.
4. Transfer the steak to a plate and let it rest for 5 minutes before serving.

COFFEE-CRUSTED SKIRT STEAK

Difficulty level: Easy

Cooking temperature: 390°F

Preparation time: 10 minutes

Cooking time: 20 minutes

Servings: 8

Ingredients:

- ¼ cup coffee beans, finely ground
- ¼ cup dark brown sugar, firmly packed
- 1 ½ tsp sea salt
- ⅛ tsp ground cinnamon
- 1 pinch of cayenne pepper
- 2 ½ lb skirt steak, cut into 4 pieces
- 1 tbsp olive oil

Directions:

1. Heat griddle to high.
2. Combine coffee, brown sugar, salt, cinnamon, and cayenne pepper in a bowl to make a rub.
3. Remove steak from refrigerator and let come to room temperature, about 15 minutes. Rub steak with oil, and sprinkle with spice rub. Massage spice rub into meat.
4. Sear until charred and medium-rare, 2–4 minutes per side. Transfer to a cutting board and cover with foil. Let it rest for 5 minutes before thinly slicing it against the grain.

MEXICAN TURKEY BURGER PATTIES

Difficulty level: Hard

Cooking temperature: 390°F

Preparation time: 10 minutes

Cooking time: 10 minutes

Servings: 4

Ingredients:

- 1 lb ground turkey
- 1 tbsp taco seasoning
- ½ cup red peppers, chopped
- ½ cup green peppers, chopped
- 1 tbsp pepper
- 1 tbsp salt

Directions:

1. Add all ingredients into the bowl and mix until well combined.
2. Preheat the griddle to high heat.
3. Spray the griddle top with cooking spray.
4. Make patties from mixture and place on hot griddle top and cook for 4–5 minutes on each side.
5. Serve and enjoy.

HERB ROASTED TURKEY

Difficulty level: Easy

Cooking temperature: 120°F

Preparation time: 15 minutes

Cooking time: 3 hours 30 minutes

Servings: 12

Ingredients:

- 14 lb turkey, cleaned
- 2 tbsp chopped mixed herbs
- 1 tbsp pork and poultry rub
- ¼ tsp ground black pepper
- 3 tbsp butter, unsalted, melted
- 8 tbsp butter, unsalted, softened
- 2 cups chicken broth

Directions:

1. Clean the turkey by removing the giblets, wash it inside out, pat dry with paper towels, place it on a roasting pan, and tuck the turkey wings by tiring it with butcher's string.
2. Turn on the griddle, set the temperature to 325°F, and let it preheat for a minimum of 15 minutes.
3. Meanwhile, prepare herb butter, and for this, take a small bowl, place the softened butter in it, add black pepper and mixed herbs and beat until fluffy.

4. Place some of the prepared herb butter underneath the skin of the turkey by using a handle of a wooden spoon, and massage the skin to distribute the butter evenly.

5. Then rub the exterior of the turkey with melted butter, season with pork and poultry rub, and pour the broth into the roasting pan.

6. When the griddle has preheated, open the lid, place the roasting pan containing turkey on the griddle grate, shut the griddle, and smoke for 3 hours and 30 minutes until the internal temperature reaches 165°F and the top has turned golden brown.

7. When done, transfer the turkey to a cutting board, let it rest for 30 minutes, then carve it into slices and serve.

FISH AND SEAFOOD RECIPES

CRISPY SKIN SALMON WITH MAPLE GINGER GLAZE

Difficulty level: Easy

Cooking temperature: 330°F

Preparation time: 10 minutes

Cooking time: 40 minutes

Servings: 4

Ingredients:

- 2 lb salmon fillets
- 1 tbsp fresh ginger
- 1 tbsp vegetable oil
- 1 tbsp Dijon mustard
- 1 tbsp salt and pepper
- ¼ cup maple syrup

Directions:

1. Prepare the ingredients.
2. Take a bowl and mix in all the ingredients except salmon fillets.
3. Coat the fillets with the mixture well.
4. Preheat the griddle.
5. Sprinkle the oil over it.
6. Place the rubbed fillets over it.
7. Sauté for 5 minutes from each side.
8. Serve and enjoy.

BACON-WRAPPED SCALLOPS

Difficulty level: Easy

Cooking temperature: 390°F

Preparation time: 10 minutes

Cooking time: 20 minutes

Servings: 4

Ingredients:

- 12 large sea scallops
- 12 toothpicks
- 8 slices bacon
- 1 tbsp vegetable oil

Direction:

1. Preheat the griddle and sauté the bacon over it.
2. Set the griddle to high.
3. With bacon, wrap the scallop and thread on the skewers.
4. Place the scallops on the griddle.
5. Serve and enjoy.

GARLIC BUTTER TILAPIA

Difficulty level: Medium

Cooking temperature: 390°F

Preparation time: 10 minutes

Cooking time: 20 minutes

Servings: 4

Ingredients:

- 2 lb tilapia fillets
- 1 tbsp salt and pepper
- 1 tsp garlic powder
- 1 tbsp butter
- ½ fresh lemon juice

Directions:

1 Mix lemon juice with butter, powder, and garlic for 10 seconds in a bowl.
2 Pour the mixture over the fillets and sprinkle the salt and pepper.
3 Preheat the griddle.
4 Sprinkle the oil on a griddle and place the filets over it.
5 Sauté them well by flipping for 4 minutes from each side.
6 Serve and enjoy.

BUTTERFIELD SHRIMP WITH SPICY MISO GLAZE

Difficulty level: Hard

Cooking temperature: 360°F

Preparation time: 10 minutes

Cooking time: 30 minutes

Servings: 4

Ingredients:

- ½ cup any miso
- 3 tbsp scallion green
- ¼ cup mirin
- 2 lb jumbo
- 1 tbsp sriracha
- 1 tbsp salt and pepper

Directions:

1. Prepare the ingredients.
2. Take a bowl and mix in all the ingredients except shrimp.
3. Put the shrimp in the mixture and rub them well to coat.
4. Preheat the griddle.
5. Sprinkle the oil over it.
6. Sauté the coated shrimp on the griddle.
7. Serve and enjoy.

COD PATTIES

Difficulty level: Easy

Cooking temperature: 350°F

Preparation time: 10 minutes

Cooking time: 12 minutes

Servings: 4

Ingredients:

- 1 egg
- 1 tbsp parsley, chopped
- 1 tbsp onion, grated
- 1 tbsp butter
- 1 lb cod fillets, cubed
- 2 potatoes, cooked, peeled, and mashed
- 1 tbsp pepper
- 1 tbsp salt

Directions:

1. Add all ingredients into the mixing bowl and mix until well combined.
2. Preheat the griddle to medium heat.
3. Spray the griddle top with cooking spray.
4. Make patties from mixture and place on hot griddle top and cook until golden brown from both sides.
5. Serve and enjoy.

GLUTEN-FREE GREMOLATA SWORDFISH SKEWERS

Difficulty level: Easy

Cooking temperature: 380°F

Preparation time: 10 minutes

Cooking time: 20 minutes

Servings: 4

Ingredients:

- 1 lb skinless swordfish fillets
- 3 lemons
- 2 tsp lemon zest
- ½ tsp red pepper flakes
- 3 tbs lemon juice
- 2 tbsp olive oil
- ½ cup parsley
- ¼ tsp black pepper
- 2 tsp garlic
- ¾ tsp sea salt

Directions:

1. Preheat the griddle.
2. Take a bowl and mix in all the ingredients except swordfish.
3. Rub in fish completely and thread on the skewers.

4. Put them down on the griddle and cook them well for 10 minutes by flipping.
5. After removing it from the griddle, sprinkle the oil on it.
6. Serve and enjoy.

SHRIMP WITH YOGURT HERB SAUCE

Difficulty level: Medium

Cooking temperature: 370°F

Preparation time: 10 minutes

Cooking time: 8 minutes

Servings: 4

Ingredients:

- 4 scallions
- 1 tbsp lemon wedges
- 2 garlic cloves
- 2 lb jumbo shrimp
- 1 small bunch of parsley
- 1 tbsp salt and pepper
- 1 cup yogurt

Directions:

1. Prepare the ingredients.
2. Take a food processor and blend in all the ingredients except shrimp.
3. Rub the shrimp in the mixture and marinate at room temperature.
4. Preheat the griddle and place the shrimp on it.
5. Sauté for 10 minutes.
6. Serve and enjoy.

BLACKENED TILAPIA

Difficulty level: Easy

Cooking temperature: 390°F

Preparation time: 10 minutes

Cooking time: 3 minutes

Servings: 4

Ingredients:

- 4 tilapia fillets
- 1 tbsp salt and pepper
- 2 tbsp butter
- ½ tsp garlic powder
- 1 tbsp olive oil
- 1 tsp oregano
- 1 tsp paprika
- ½ tsp ground cumin
- 1 lemon

Directions:

1. Take a bowl and mix in all the ingredients.
2. Rub the fish in the ingredients.
3. Preheat the griddle.
4. Melt the butter on the griddle and place the fillets on the griddle.
5. Cook them for 3 minutes.
6. Serve and enjoy.

QUICK AND DELICIOUS HALIBUT

Difficulty level: Easy

Cooking temperature: 380°F

Preparation time: 10 minutes

Cooking time: 10 minutes

Servings: 2

Ingredients:

- 2 halibut fish fillets
- 2 tsp olive oil
- 1 tsp dried thyme
- ½ tsp onion powder
- ¾ tsp garlic powder
- 1 tbsp paprika
- ¼ tsp salt

Directions:

1. In a small bowl, mix paprika, garlic powder, onion powder, thyme, and salt.
2. Brush fish fillets with oil and rub with spice mixture.
3. Preheat the griddle to high heat.
4. Spray the griddle top with cooking spray.
5. Place fish fillets on a hot griddle top and cook for 3–5 minutes on each side.
6. Serve and enjoy.

LEMON-PEPPER SCALLOPS

Difficulty level: Medium

Cooking temperature: 390°F

Preparation time: 10 minutes

Cooking time: 6 minutes

Servings: 4

Ingredients:

- 20 scallops
- 1 ½ tbsp lemon-pepper seasoning
- 4 tbsp olive oil
- 1 tsp salt

Directions:

1. Add scallops and remaining ingredients into the mixing bowl and mix well and place in the refrigerator for 30 minutes.
2. Preheat the griddle to high heat.
3. Place scallops on a hot griddle top and cooks for 2–3 minutes on each side.
4. Serve and enjoy.

HEALTHY SALMON PATTIES

Difficulty level: Easy

Cooking temperature: 370°F

Preparation time: 10 minutes

Cooking time: 10 minutes

Servings: 6

Ingredients:

- 2 eggs
- 15 oz can salmon, bones removed
- 2 tbsp green onion, chopped
- 2 tbsp mayonnaise
- 1 small bell pepper, chopped
- ½ cup breadcrumbs
- ⅓ cup Parmesan cheese, shredded
- 1 tbsp pepper
- 1 tbsp salt

Directions:

1. Add all ingredients into the mixing bowl and mix until well combined.
2. Preheat the griddle to medium heat.
3. Spray the griddle top with cooking spray.
4. Make patties from mixture and place on hot griddle top and cook for 5 minutes on each side.
5. Serve and enjoy.

CHIPOTLE SALMON

Difficulty level: Hard

Cooking temperature: 390°F

Preparation time: 10 minutes

Cooking time: 15 minutes

Servings: 4

Ingredients:

- 4 salmon fillets
- 1 ¼ tsp chipotle powder
- ½ tbsp ground cumin
- 1 tbsp brown sugar
- 1 tsp salt

Directions:

1. In a small bowl, mix chipotle powder, cumin, brown sugar, and salt and sprinkle over salmon fillets.
2. Preheat the griddle to high heat.
3. Spray the griddle top with cooking spray.
4. Place salmon fillets on a hot griddle top and cook for 10–15 minutes or until cooked.
5. Serve and enjoy.

MOUTHWATERING LEMON SCALLOPS WITH GARLIC

Difficulty level: Medium

Cooking temperature: 370°F

Preparation time: 10 minutes

Cooking time: 5 minutes

Servings: 2

Ingredients:

- 1 lb frozen bay scallops, thawed, rinsed, and pat dry
- 1 tsp garlic, minced
- 2 tbsp olive oil
- 1 tsp parsley, chopped
- 1 tsp lemon juice
- 1 tbsp pepper
- 1 tbsp salt

Directions:

1. 1. Preheat the griddle to high heat. Add oil to the griddle top.
2. Add garlic and sauté for 30 seconds.
3. Add scallops, lemon juice, pepper, and salt, then sauté until scallops turn opaque.
4. Garnish with parsley and serve.

FLAVORFUL TILAPIA

Difficulty level: Hard

Cooking temperature: 380°F

Preparation time: 10 minutes

Cooking time: 8 minutes

Servings: 4

Ingredients:

- 4 tilapia fillets
- 1 tsp garlic powder
- 2 tsp paprika
- 3 tbsp olive oil
- ½ tsp pepper
- 1tsp salt

Directions:

1. Brush fish fillets with oil and season with garlic powder, paprika, pepper, and salt.
2. Preheat the griddle to high heat.
3. Spray the griddle top with cooking spray.
4. Place fish fillets on a hot griddle top and cook for 4 minutes on each side. Enjoy!

GARLIC HADDOCK

Difficulty level: Easy

Cooking temperature: 390°F

Preparation time: 10 minutes

Cooking time: 10 minutes

Servings: 4

Ingredients:

- 4 haddock fish fillets
- 2 tbsp garlic, minced
- 2 tbsp olive oil
- 1tbsp salt

Directions:

1. Brush fish fillets with oil and season with garlic and salt.
2. Preheat the griddle to high heat.
3. Spray the griddle top with cooking spray.
4. Place fish fillets on a hot griddle top and cook for 4–5 minutes on each side.

LEMON GARLIC SHRIMP

Difficulty level: Easy

Cooking temperature: 390°F

Preparation time: 15–20 minutes

Cooking time: 15 minutes

Servings: 4

Ingredients:

- 1 ½ lb shrimp, peeled and deveined
- 1 tbsp garlic, minced
- ¼ cup butter
- ¼ cup fresh parsley, chopped
- ¼ cup fresh lemon juice
- 1 tbsp pepper
- 1 tbsp salt

Directions:

1. Preheat the griddle to high heat.
2. Melt butter on the griddle top.
3. Add garlic and sauté for 30 seconds.
4. Add shrimp and season with pepper and salt and cook for 4–5 minutes or until it turns pink.
5. Add lemon juice and parsley and stir well and cook for 2 minutes.
6. Serve and enjoy.

SHRIMP ON THE BARBIE

Difficulty level: Hard

Cooking temperature: 320°F

Preparation time: 15–20 minutes

Cooking time: 55 minutes

Servings: 4

Ingredients:

- 3 lb large raw shrimp, peeled and deveined
- ½ lb butter, melted
- 3 garlic cloves, minced
- Zest and juice of 1 lemon
- 2 tsp sea salt
- 2 tsp black pepper
- ¼ cup grated Parmesan cheese

Directions:

1. Place the shrimp on skewers.
2. Mix the remaining ingredients and set in a bowl.
3. Heat the griddle grill high and grill the shrimp, brushing with the butter mixture, for 2 minutes per side until cooked through. They will be solid in color with white and pink tones rather than blue and gray.
4. Serve with grilled summer vegetables, grilled yellow potatoes, or grilled corn.

LEMON PEPPER TROUT

Difficulty level: Easy

Cooking temperature: 390°F

Preparation time: 10 minutes **Cooking time:** 10 minutes

Servings: 2

Ingredients:

- 2 trout fillets
- 2 tsp lemon juice
- 2 tbsp lemon pepper seasoning

Directions:

1   Season fish fillets with lemon pepper seasoning.
2   Preheat the griddle to medium heat.
3   Spray the griddle top with cooking spray.
4   Place fish fillets on a hot griddle top and cook for 5–10 minutes.
5   Drizzle with lemon juice and serve.

OREGANO SHRIMP SKEWERS

Difficulty level: Easy

Cooking temperature: 370°F

Preparation time: 10 minutes

Cooking time: 7 minutes

Servings: 6

Ingredients:

- 1 ½ lb shrimp, peeled and deveined
- 1 tbsp dried oregano
- 2 tsp garlic paste
- 2 lemons juice
- ¼ cup olive oil
- 1 tsp paprika
- 1 tbsp pepper
- 1 tbsp salt

Directions:

1. Add all ingredients into the mixing bowl, mix well, and place in the refrigerator for 1 hour.
2. Remove marinated shrimp from the refrigerator and thread it onto the skewers.
3. Preheat the griddle to high heat.
4. Place skewers onto the griddle top and cook for 5–7 minutes.
5. Serve and enjoy.

FLAVORFUL BALSAMIC SALMON

Difficulty level: Hard

Cooking temperature: 390°F

Preparation time: 10 minutes

Cooking time: 10 minutes

Servings: 6

Ingredients:

- 6 salmon fillets
- 5 tbsp balsamic vinaigrette
- 2 tbsp olive oil
- 1 ½ tsp garlic powder
- 1 tbsp pepper
- 1 tbsp salt

Directions:

1. In a mixing bowl, add salmon, garlic powder, balsamic vinaigrette, pepper, and salt, and mix well. Set aside.
2. Preheat the griddle to high heat.
3. Add oil to the hot griddle top.
4. Place salmon onto the griddle top and cook for 3–5 minutes on each side or until cooked.
5. Serve and enjoy.

SARDINES WITH LEMON AND THYME

Difficulty level: Easy

Cooking temperature: 390°F

Preparation time: 10 minutes

Cooking time: 8 minutes

Servings: 4

Ingredients:

- 1 lb fresh sardines
- 4 lemon wedges
- 1 tbsp good quality olive oil
- 1 small bunch of thyme
- 1 tbsp salt and pepper

Directions:

1. Prepare the ingredients.
2. Sprinkle the olive oil on the fish and spread the salt and pepper over it.
3. Preheat the griddle.
4. Cook the fish on the grill for 8 minutes.
5. Serve and enjoy.

GLUTEN-FREE BLACKENED SALMON

Difficulty level: Easy

Cooking temperature: 380°F

Preparation time: 15–20 minutes

Cooking time: 10 minutes

Servings: 4

Ingredients:

- ¼ lb salmon fillets
- 2 tbsp blackened seasoning
- 2 tbsp butter

Directions:

1   Season salmon fillets with blackened seasoning.
2   Preheat the griddle to high heat.
3   Melt butter on the griddle top.
4   Place salmon fillets onto the hot griddle top and cook for 4–5 minutes.
5   Turn the salmon and cook for 4–5 minutes more.
6   Serve and enjoy.

ITALIAN SHRIMP

Difficulty level: Easy

Cooking temperature: 390°F

Preparation time: 15–20 minutes

Cooking time: 5 minutes

Servings: 4

Ingredients:

- 1 lb shrimp, deveined
- 1 tsp Italian seasoning
- 1 tsp paprika
- 1 ½ tsp garlic, minced
- 1 stick butter
- 1 fresh lemon juice
- ¼ tsp pepper
- ½ tsp salt

Directions:

1. Preheat the griddle to high heat.
2. Melt butter on the hot griddle top.
3. Add garlic and cook for 30 seconds.
4. Toss shrimp with paprika, Italian seasoning, pepper, and salt.
5. Add shrimp into the pan and cook for 2–3 minutes per side.
6. Drizzle lemon juice over the shrimp.
7. Stir and serve.

VEGETABLES RECIPES

EASY SEARED GREEN BEANS

Difficulty level: Medium

Preparation time: 10 minutes

Cooking time: 10 minutes

Servings: 6

Ingredients:

- 1 ½ lb green bean, trimmed
- 1 ½ tbsp rice vinegar
- 3 tbsp soy sauce
- 1 ½ tbsp sesame oil
- 2 tbsp sesame seeds, toasted
- 1 ½ tbsp brown sugar
- ¼ tsp black pepper

Directions:

1. Cook green beans in boiling water for 3 minutes and drain well.
2. Transfer green beans to chilled ice water and drain again. Pat dry green beans.
3. Preheat the griddle to high heat.
4. Add oil to the hot griddle top.
5. Add green beans and stir fry for 2 minutes.
6. Add soy sauce, brown sugar, vinegar, and pepper and stir fry for 2 minutes more.
7. Add sesame seeds and toss well to coat.
8. Serve and enjoy.

HASH POTATOES WITH ONION AND BELL PEPPERS

Difficulty level: Easy

Preparation time: 10 minutes

Cooking time: 17 minutes

Servings: 4

Ingredients:

- 4 large potatoes, peeled and cut into ½-inch cubes
- 1 red bell pepper, chopped
- 3 garlic cloves, minced
- 1 onion, chopped
- 1 tbsp unsalted butter
- ¼ cup olive oil
- 2 tsp fresh parsley, chopped
- ¼ cup Parmesan cheese, grated
- 1 tbsp pepper and salt

Directions:

1. Preheat the griddle and add oil and butter. 2. Add potatoes and mix well to coat the oil.
2. Cover it and let it cook for 10 minutes at medium heat.
3. Remove the lid and add bell pepper and onions; mix well.
4. Cook for 15 minutes while stirring occasionally.
5. Add garlic, pepper, salt, and parsley, and cook for 2 minutes.
6. Sprinkle with Parmesan cheese. Serve and enjoy!

DELICIOUS BROCCOLI ON GRIDDLE

Difficulty level: Easy

Preparation time: 10 minutes

Cooking time: 12 minutes

Servings: 4

Ingredients:

- 4 cups broccoli florets
- 1 ¼ tsp salt
- ¼ tsp black pepper
- 1 tbsp lemon juice
- 1 ½ tsp Italian seasonings
- 1 ½ tsp minced garlic

Directions:

1. Take all the ingredients to a bowl.
2. Mix well.
3. Cover with plastic wrap.
4. Keep in refrigerator for 1 hour. 5 Preheat the griddle.
6. Drizzle some oil over a griddle.
7. Spread the marinated broccoli over the griddle and cook until golden brown.
8. Serve and enjoy!

GARLIC PARMESAN ASPARAGUS

Difficulty level: Easy

Preparation time: 10 minutes

Cooking time: 10 minutes

Servings: 4

Ingredients:

- 1 lb fresh asparagus
- 3 tbsp Parmesan cheese, shaved
- 2 tbsp olive oil
- 1 tbsp sea salt
- 2 garlic cloves, minced
- 1 tbsp black pepper

Directions:

1. Preheat the griddle.
2. Trim off the bottoms of asparagus.
3. Take a baking sheet, place asparagus on it, toss in olive oil, and season with pepper & salt.
4. Place asparagus on the griddle and cook for 5–10 minutes until they tendered.
5. Add garlic and toss.
6. Add Parmesan cheese.

STIR VEGETABLES WITH LEMON SCALLION

Difficulty level: Medium

Preparation time: 10 minutes

Cooking time: 12 minutes

Servings: 4

Ingredients:

- ½ cup bell peppers, cut into cubes of 1-inch
- ½ cup zucchini, cut into cubes of 1-inch
- ½ cup yellow squash, sliced into a cube of 1-inch chunks
- ½ cup button mushrooms
- ½ cup red onion, cut into cubes of 1-inch
- 1 tsp black pepper
- ½ cup cherry tomatoes
- 3 tbsp olive oil
- 1 tsp sea salt

For the lemon vinaigrette:

- 2 scallions, sliced
- 1 ½ lemon, juiced
- 1 tsp lemon zest
- ¼ tsp honey
- 1 tbsp champagne/ white wine vinegar
- 1 tbsp olive oil

Directions:

1. Preheat the griddle and add oil to it.
2. Put vegetables on the griddle.
3. Please put it on the griddle and cook from both sides for 5 minutes.
4. Mix ingredients of lemon vinaigrette in a bowl.
5. Drizzle with a mixture of lemon vinaigrette.
6. Serve and enjoy!

GLUTEN-FREE SAUTÉED PEPPERS

Difficulty level: Hard

Preparation time: 10 minutes

Cooking time: 10 minutes

Servings: 4

Ingredients:

- 1 red bell pepper,
- 1 green bell pepper
- 1 sweet yellow onion, chopped
- ½ tsp salt
- 1 tbsp vegetable oil

Directions:

1. Remove seeds of red bell pepper and green bell peppers, and cut them into half-inch strips.
2. Preheat the griddle and add oil to it.
3. Add peppers and onions, and sprinkle salt.
4. Stir for 3–7 minutes.
5. Serve and enjoy!

VEGGIE YAKISOBA

Difficulty level: Medium

Preparation time: 15–30 minutes

Cooking time: 8 minutes

Servings: 4

Ingredients:

- 2 tbsp soy sauce
- 2 tbsp mirin
- 1 tsp sesame oil
- 2 tsp garlic, minced
- 2 tbsp brown sugar
- ½ tsp ground ginger
- 3 tbsp rapeseed oil
- ½ cup sliced onion
- 1 sliced bell pepper
- 1 cup broccoli
- 1 cup sliced zucchini
- ½ cup matchstick carrots
- 17 oz yakisoba noodles

Directions:

1. Mix the first 6 ingredients in a bowl and set aside.
2. Preheat the griddle and heat the rapeseed oil.
3. Sauté the onion for 2 minutes.

4. Stir in the bell pepper, broccoli, zucchini, and carrots. Stir for 3 minutes until wilted.

5. Add the noodles and stir for another 2 minutes.

6. Pour in the sauce and cook for another minute.

GRILLED VEGGIE SALAD

Difficulty level: Hard

Preparation time: 15–30 minutes

Cooking time: 10 minutes

Servings: 5

Ingredients:

- 2 small zucchinis, cut lengthwise
- 1 corn on the cob, sliced
- 1 sweet bell pepper, seeded
- 1 tbsp olive oil
- 1 tbsp salt and pepper to taste
- 1 onion, sliced
- 2 large tomatoes, chopped
- 4 tbsp grated Parmesan cheese
- 2 tbsp balsamic vinegar
- ½ cup torn basil leaves

Directions:

1. Preheat the griddle and heat the oil.
2. Brush zucchini, corn, and bell pepper with olive oil and season with salt and pepper to taste.
3. Place zucchini, corn, and bell pepper on the griddle pan. Grill for 3–5 minutes on each side.
4. For the corn, remove the kernels from the cob.

5. Place all ingredients in a bowl and toss to coat everything with the seasonings.

GLUTEN-FREE MEDITERRANEAN GRILLED VEGGIES

Difficulty level: Easy

Preparation time: 15–30 minutes

Cooking time: 10 minutes

Servings: 4

Ingredients:

- 2 zucchinis, sliced
- 1 eggplant, sliced
- 3 Roma tomatoes, sliced
- 12 mini peppers
- 8 oz Brussels sprouts
- 2 lemons, juiced
- ¼ cup olive oil
- 1 tsp sumac
- 1 tbsp salt and pepper

Directions:

1. Preheat the griddle and heat the oil.
2. Place the first 5 ingredients in a bowl and toss to coat the vegetables with the seasoning.
3. Grill for 3–5 minutes for each side.
4. Meanwhile, mix the olive oil, sumac, salt, and pepper.

BELL PEPPER BROCCOLI SAUTÉ

Difficulty level: Easy

Preparation time: 10 minutes

Cooking time: 30 minutes

Servings: 4

Ingredients:

- 1 cup yellow bell pepper (cut into small pieces)
- 5 cups broccoli florets
- 2 tbsp garlic, chopped
- 1 tbsp sesame seeds, toasted
- ¼ cup water

Directions:

1. Preheat the griddle and add butter to melt.
2. Add garlic, bell pepper, and broccoli.
3. Cook for 3 minutes while stirring occasionally.
4. Add water, cover, and reduce heat to medium.
5. Cook for 4 minutes or till broccoli is tender.
6. Sprinkle sesame seeds.
7. Serve and enjoy!

ROASTED SWEET PEPPERS

Difficulty level: Medium

Preparation time: 10 minutes

Cooking time: 12 minutes

Servings: 4

Ingredients:

- 1 tbsp olive oil
- 1 lb sweet peppers (mini)
- ¼ tsp salt

Directions:

1. Remove peppers stem, cut lengthwise into half, and remove seeds.
2. Preheat the griddle.
3. Add oil.
4. Add peppers and sprinkle salt.
5. Cook for 8 minutes while occasionally stirring until softened.
6. Serve and enjoy!

ROASTED CARROTS

Difficulty level: Hard

Preparation time: 10 minutes

Cooking time: 15 minutes

Servings: 4

Ingredients:

- 1 lb carrots (peeled and cut into pieces)
- 1 tbsp olive oil
- ½ cup water
- ¼ tsp salt

Directions:

1. Preheat the griddle skillet.
2. Add water and salt, then put in the carrots.
3. Cook covered for 8 minutes until carrots are tender.
4. When water is dissolved, add oil and cook for 2–3 minutes while stirring occasionally.
5. Serve and enjoy!

GRIDDLED SUMMER VEGETABLES

Difficulty level: Easy

Preparation time: 15–30 minutes

Cooking time: 6 minutes

Servings: 4

Ingredients:

- 1 tbsp olive oil
- 1 cup asparagus spears, cleaned
- 1 large eggplant, sliced
- 1 zucchini, sliced
- 1 fennel bulb, sliced
- Juice of ½ lemon
- 1 tbsp salt and pepper to taste

Directions:

1. Heat the griddle pan to medium and brush with oil.
2. Place the vegetables on the griddle pan.
3. Season with lemon juice, salt, and pepper.
4. Cook until the vegetables are roasted.

BEST GRILLED CARROTS

Difficulty level: Easy

Preparation time: 15–30 minutes **Cooking time:** 10 minutes

Servings: 3

Ingredients:

- 1 ½ lb large carrots, cut lengthwise
- 1 tbsp olive oil
- ½ tsp salt
- 1 tbsp chopped cilantro
- ½ lime, juiced
- ¼ tsp ground cumin

Directions:

1. Preheat the griddle and heat the oil.
2. Place all ingredients in a bowl and toss to coat the carrots with the seasoning.
3. Grill the carrots for 6–10 minutes.

GLUTEN-FREE POLENTA WITH ROSEMARY

Difficulty level: Easy

Preparation time: 5 minutes

Cooking time: 10 minutes

Servings: 4–6

Ingredients:

- 24 oz log-prepared polenta
- 2 tsp extra-virgin olive oil
- 1 tbsp garlic salt to taste
- 1 tbsp lemon-pepper seasoning to taste
- 2 tbsp chopped rosemary

Directions:

1   Preheat the griddle to high. Cut the polenta into 12½-inch thick slices. Place the slices on a baking sheet.

2   Brush both sides of the polenta rounds with oil and season lightly with garlic salt, lemon pepper seasoning, and sprinkle with chopped rosemary leaves.

3   Lightly oil the grill rack and grill your polenta slices over high heat until nicely browned, within 3–5 minutes per side. Remove from heat and serve on a heated platter.